Everyone Has

UNSOLICITED ADVICE FOR BEING HUMAN

SH T

JESSICA LEIGH LEVIN

ALSO BY JESSICA LEIGH LEVIN

PERFECT PAIRINGS: THE ART OF CONNECTING PEOPLE

REVIEWS

Want an action-driven plan for getting through the worst that life might just have to offer? Jessica Levin's second book, Everyone Has Sh*t: Unsolicited Advice for Being Human, *does just that. Blending interviews with personal stories, accounts of success and heartbreak, and chapter-end lists of actionable steps to help deal with sh*t or overcome it, Levin lifts the hood on the social veneer that keeps us all presentable in society. The result is an honest account on how to deal with the very personal challenges of self-confidence, disappointing relationships, and self-serving advice by others. Life is not easy, Levin explains. But there are ways of dealing with hardship that let us keep our heads high as we walk through life. In other words, her book is a very worthwhile read.*

— *Jay Lemming, Author*

We live an in an era that demands that we always act like things are fine, everything is under control, we lead happy and fulfilling lives—sometimes just in exchange for a few likes on Facebook or Instagram. Everybody has advice, everybody wants us to teach us how to live. What I love about this book is that it is an un-guide to being yourself—an incredibly simple tool that encourages you to invest in what really matters: yourself. Whether you are struggling with your next work move or trying to get ahead in life, this is a must read, to offload your brain and soul, and focus on your life."

—*Julius Solaris, Event Manager Blog*

*"Everyone Has Sh*t: Unsolicited Advice for Being Human is one of the few books that as soon as I started reading it—I couldn't stop! Not only does Jessica give real-life examples that show just how much sh*t we all deal with but she gives great advice on how to deal with it in a practical and HUMAN way. Your sh*t may be different than hers or mine, but we all have to deal with it. This book was a refreshing and humorous look on how we can all better ourselves along the journey. I highly recommend reading it yourself and maybe a few copies for friends that may need a little encouragement.*

—*Lynette Young, Speaker, Author*

Everyone Has Sh*t:
Unsolicited Advice for Being Human

Library of Congress Control Number: 2017916266

Cover Design by Karen Houser Design
Cover Illustration by Boris Zhitkov

Published by
Emerald Publishing, LLC
97 Main Street
Woodbridge, NJ 07095
emeraldpublishingcompany.com

ISBN-13: 978-0-9861692-2-9

For Isaiah, Pearl, Joyce and Logan

May you have minimal shit in your lives
and sometimes take the unsolicited advice
of your Auntie Jessica.

Also, please remember when I'm old and senile,
that I once dedicated a book to you.

Acknowledgements

The best things in my life are the people who support me. I have the best cheerleaders on the planet and am eternally grateful to each and every one.

Shelley Harland-Wright, thank you for encouraging me to change the title of the book and keep it real. That little push made all the difference.

Karen Houser, for an amazing cover and great friendship.

Wesley Sullivan, who made sure I finished writing during our vacation and who loves me despite my shit.

Stacy Hanas, who helped me get this out the door to the world and generally puts up with my insanity and endless stories.

Deborah Pannell, who pushed me over the finish line. Without her compassion and fierce editing skills, this book wouldn't exist.

Amber Marlow, for teaching me to be more sensitive. Your activism is not unnoticed.

Howard Konicov, who is always my cheerleader and friend.

Andy Falter, who is always good for a pep talk.

Joey Passion and Samantha Granados, who took my photos and made me up for my beautiful headshot.

Deb Roth, who is always there.

Lina Trubilla, for having a kind spirit that everyone should embody.

Saira Banu Kianes, for extraordinary kindness and for bringing me wine when I've needed it.

Noelle Stary, for calling me every morning before we get our days started.

Carree Olshansky Musgrove, for Spring Break OH-9 and the almost 30 years of friendship.

#RAS Ladies, you know who you are. Thank you for being a sounding board for life's shit.

Everyone who has taught me a lesson or broken my heart. You made me stronger. You made me better.

Table of Contents

Foreword

"Sometimes you need to wear an epic dress and dance your ass off barefoot in a Vegas pool."

That, in a nutshell, is Jessica Levin.

Imagine waking up in the morning, checking your Facebook feed, and seeing this little burst of enthusiasm from one of the most positive individuals you have ever known—yet someone whom you have never actually met.

That's the type of thing that you'll see on your feed when you are Jessica's friend on Facebook. You'll find posts that will inspire you, make you laugh, cheer with enthusiasm, or ponder your current state in the world. During the darkest days of the 2016 US election, when many came to realize that the world was in for a period of time that would challenge their mood and optimism on a regular basis, Jessica decided to do a daily post of a section of the US Constitution—perhaps to remind people that in an era of darkest negativity, there was always a path forward.

I'm honoured to be a friend of Jessica, even though our physical paths have not crossed! We've tried to actually meet during our various voyages on the road, but it has never come about. Even so, I feel like I know her well—her moods, her joys, her activities, her inspirations, and yes, her challenges.

And with that, I am honoured that she reached out to me to write an introduction to her book—one that would be fitting of the positive message that she brings to those who are burdened with challenges.

Everyone has challenges—all of us share the occasional awfulness of being. Everyone has known, at one time or another, the depths of despair that can come from some sort of dreadful burden. I know that Jessica has faced issues along her remarkable voyage in life and work—and yet, she lives life to the fullest, eager to tell the world that she would rather seek out the moments of joy than wallow in periodic moments of pain.

To share in Jessica's life is to know that there is always something positive to be found. I am inspired when I see a message from one of her staff praising Jessica for her mentorship—and know that she has touched many lives simply by caring, teaching, training and challenging. When faced with yet the latest in a string of never-ending natural disasters, Jessica is right there with her efforts to alleviate suffering through her efforts with Operation BBQ Relief. When interrupted in her life by some complex and challenging situation, she instantly shares the joy she finds in one of her nieces. And those of us who watch her from afar cheer when we often see her win some well-earned award or recognition for the work that she is doing in the event and communications world.

To spend time near Jessica is to also learn the magic of online, collaborative communications. Just this morning, she posted a question requesting tips on effective strategies for moving—and I know that she will, in an instant, have dozens of tips from those who are also her friends.

To be a futurist and a speaker is to be someone who has to regularly learn to say no—there are too many potential events, too little time, and too many requests. You manage your life through the fee that you set. That said, one of the most difficult 'no's' in my 25-year career was when I had to say 'no' to Jessica.

She approached me, a bubble of enthusiasm, to be the opening keynote speaker for an event that she was managing in New Orleans. Simply put, the client didn't have the fee that is required, and I really, really, really had to say no. It was hard, because I knew that it would be a stellar event, full of innovative ideas, activities and content. And I must say, it was really hard to watch the Twitter stream for the event from afar, because you could see that she pulled together something remarkable.

What defines Jessica is this: she won't hold a grudge against you for your decisions—she will understand the reasons behind them, and she will find another path. She'll find a way to turn that challenge into an opportunity. In my own case, I know that she'll come back to me again some time in the future with another opportunity, and so I know that my 'no' will at one point turn to a 'yes.'

That's the thing. Jessica is relentlessly optimistic, always focused on opportunity and eager to communicate her enthusiasm. In this book, she is eager to share what has brought her this remarkable quality. It is a human trait that all of us should possess.

That's why you should read this book.

To be in Jessica's orbit is to be in proximity to the energy of a star of positivity, at the same tie that a black hole of negative challenges might spell doom. In this book, may you discover some waves of positive gravity that will light you up, inspire you, and help you to always focus on the goodness in your life!

Jim Carroll
Futurist

Introduction

Life is good. I have a business, a tremendous network of friends and, much of the time, the aptitude to make smart decisions. I am blessed with the ability to find answers and solve problems. Some of this is an innate skill; a lot of it is learned. But this doesn't mean that life is easy. It's always an uphill battle that requires careful planning and thought to reach the summit. Even people who appear to "have it all" struggle. Oprah. Richard Branson. Mark Cuban. Do I know this because I asked them or read one of the many biographies about their lives? No. It's because we are all human and life is a series of ups, downs and all arounds. Those who are the most successful have a better understanding of how to navigate it: where to get help, how to leverage the simple act of kindness, and most of all, when to ask for advice.

Even superheroes have shit. In fact, they are the epitome of triumphing over adversity. Superman is an orphan who leads a double life and hides his identity from his girlfriend for much of their relationship. But in true superhero fashion, he focuses on his strength (literally) and is dedicated to making the world a better place.

This book is designed to do one thing: *make your life better*. While this is my second book, it was the first one I wanted to write. By contrast, I wrote "Perfect Pairings: The Art of Connecting People" on the advice of a dear friend and a trusted colleague. It was the right decision for me at the time, and a reminder that the advice of trusted friends is invaluable. We cannot do this thing we call life alone.

I'm not a psychologist, and I wouldn't even call myself an expert (don't stop reading yet). I am someone who meets a lot of people and has many conversations. I cross paths with people from different walks of life. I've had my share of ups and downs, and I'm still learning.

The stories here are deeply personal, but I share them in hopes that others can benefit. Lessons come from living and everyone has experiences to share. This book is full of anecdotes. Use them as a guide. No one can make choices for you, but having knowledge and insight often brings clarity.

Reading this book is the beginning of a journey. It lays the foundation for a more fulfilled and richer life. The book is not a magic bean. On the day that you finish reading it, you won't miraculously wake up and have the perfect life of your dreams. Instead, you will have perspective and tools. Each chapter in this book covers a different facet of life. Absorb, reflect upon and integrate the examples into your daily existence. At the end of this book, you will have a guide to being awesome, and you'll understand: Everyone has shit.

One note: For many of the personal stories in this book, I have changed the names to resemble those of fictional cartoon characters. For interviews or less personal tales, I have used real names. You'll figure this out as we go.

EVERYONE HAS SHIT

"Part of my act is meant to shake you up.
It looks like I'm being funny, but I'm reminding you
of other things. Life is tough, darling. Life is hard.
And we better laugh at everything; otherwise,
we're going down the tube."

– Joan Rivers

In high school, I ran for student council seven times and lost...seven times. My campaign slogan on that last run was "Don't Make it Seven, Vote Jessica Levin." It's true—you can laugh. Not quite the captain of the cheerleading squad or homecoming queen, I struggled to make friends, and my family life was unstable.

As an adult, my life has also had its challenges—a slew of medical issues that, while not life-threatening, caused me significant physical pain for many years. Would the average person who meets me know that? Nope. Do you want to know why? Because everyone has their own shit that they are dealing with, and they don't need to hear about mine.

I embrace my shit. It's mine, and I own it. Once you recognize that perfect lives do not exist, and that humans are innately complicated, your perspective shifts. People are complex. Say it with me and remember it. People are complex. Everyone is dealing with something, and even the most logical and "put-together" person has something that is unsettled for them. It's the essence of humanity.

There is a laundry list of successful people who have overcome significant obstacles to lead exemplary and enviable lives. Their stories embody the cliché, "What doesn't kill you makes you stronger." When you're going through hard times, that's the last thing you want to hear, but there's real truth to it. Obstacles need to be navigated, or you come to a dead stop. Obstacles can be a blessing. They drive us and give us reasons to push forward. They also give us reasons to be thankful.

Did you know that being grateful is a common trait among successful people? Practicing gratitude on a daily basis also makes it easier to deal with the daily shit. Throughout this book we'll discuss being thankful, even in the moments that hurt the most.

Let's not diminish the seriousness of some obstacles. In life, we face some very serious setbacks. Illness (our own or a family member's), financial difficulties, divorce, addiction, etc. can consume us and put us in hard-to-recover-from situations. Even with hurdles, somehow, I learned that obstacles are not permanent limitations, and I'm the only person who can hold me back in life. This is not about casually dismissing life's challenges, but managing them, so we can rebound faster and come back better.

> **LESSONS FOR BEING HUMAN**
>
> 1. Going into the game understanding that everyone has shit in their lives is the first step. Just because it looks easy for someone doesn't mean that it is. It's not. I promise you, it's not.
>
> 2. Shit happens. Own it.
>
> 3. People are complex. To pretend otherwise would be an insult to humanity.
>
> 4. Practice gratitude. Laugh. Keep trying—seven or eight times.
>
> 5. Everyone has shit.

TAKE MY ADVICE, I'M NOT USING IT

"The best way to give advice to your children is to find out what they want and then advise them to do it."

– Harry S. Truman

I'm publishing this book for my 40th birthday. I don't feel old, but more like a perfectly ripened avocado. A little rough on the outside, but silky soft on the inside in a way that is luxurious and mature. OK, enough about me being an avocado. The point is that in my 40 years on this planet, I have gained some wisdom and perspective. Here's what I know...

- The best possible scenario for one person is not always best for another.
- Our personal experiences vary greatly, and no one else goes through them the same way we do.
- No one is completely objective. Our opinions are often filtered through such factors as socioeconomic status. That doesn't make our opinions any more or less valid than anyone else's, just different.
- Our families influence our opinions, but their perspectives are based on their unique experiences, and they are not always right for us.
- We can be right and wrong at the same time. Life is filled with gray area.
- Although we should understand the generally accepted concepts of right and wrong, we still need our inner compass to navigate them. Remember that at one time, slavery was legal, women couldn't vote and cigarettes were marketed as healthy. And we are still a long way from a perfectly just and equitable society.

I have traveled to other countries and spent time with people who are very different from me. I have friends whose lives are much harder than mine. The last several years have brought me exponential gains in insight. Perhaps it's just a function of how life works, or perhaps I have become more reflective, but I have felt an internal shift that has prepared me to write this book.

Believe it or not, I do not have all the answers. Recently, I read an internet meme highlighting advice from "old people." My interpretation of old meant people above the age of 80, but then again, my 16-year-old nephew thinks I'm old at 40. That's perspective for you.

One quote in the meme resonated with me more than others. It said, "It is perfectly fine to accept and solicit advice from other people, maybe even a handful of people. However, at the end of the day, the only advice that you can really take is your own."

We all have friends and family who will try to convince us that they are right. I'm guilty of this too, especially when I feel passionately about an issue. I mean really, I wrote a book about "unsolicited advice." But even I realize that, as advice givers, whether we like it or not, we must accept that people are responsible for their own actions and mistakes. People must face the consequences of their decisions. Give and take advice, but ultimately, an individual owns her life's experiences.

Nancy is an advice seeker—especially during stressful situations. She will have conversation after conversation, seeking a solution. Some of her "advisors" give her the answer they think she wants to hear, while others give her the one that makes them feel best about themselves. Here's a shocker: People don't always give you advice with the purest of intentions. More often than not, this is done subconsciously and they don't necessarily mean harm. Factors like jealousy may find their way into the advice, leaving it tainted and diluted.

Nancy often perceives the people whom she seeks out for advice as being smarter than she is. She equates more experience with intelligence. They are not the same thing. She once described a conversation with a colleague who advised her to close her company and get a "real job." My response was, "You know what? He's right. Forget everything that you have worked hard to accomplish. Pack it up, go home and get a job, because someone who has peripheral knowledge of your business said you should."

My sarcasm was meant to emphasize just how ridiculous the advice she received sounded. Leveraging wisdom can be phenomenal. Another angle often brings clarity or new ideas. But in the end, it's important to use your own judgment. Your job, as a human, is to assimilate all the sagacity you receive and to come to your own unique conclusion—the conclusion that is best for you and your situation.

Rachel S. Heslin has been immersed in the study of human psychology for more than 35 years. She authored "Navigating Life: 8 Different Strategies to Guide Your Way." She has some interesting advice on, well, advice:

"Learn how to identify when you are doing something that isn't really yours to do. Human beings are naturally social creatures: we continuously adjust our perspectives, choices, and behavior based on our interactions with others. This is generally a positive trait that helps us develop community and strengthens our relationships.

"However, we too often allow the social validation of doing what others expect of us to override our own innate skills, talents, and perspectives. If we're constantly doing what we think we should do instead of what we want to do, not only are we less happy, but we're less productive, because our hearts aren't in it.

"When I talk about shoulds, I'm not referring to personal discipline. It's very useful to develop the discipline to take care of what needs to be done in order to accomplish larger goals. I'm referring to a should that's attached to the larger goal, itself.

"For example, say your father has his own CPA firm and expects you to take over the family business. You are expected to become an accountant and learn how to run a CPA firm. However, if what you really want to do is become a teacher, then even if you are quite capable of becoming an excellent accountant, doing so would be an inefficient use—a waste—of your true calling."

Heslin makes a great case for learning how to define our personal priorities from within. While it's good to learn from and engage with others in dialogue as we work through our shit, ultimately, as we make our decisions, we have to learn how to rely on our own judgment.

LESSONS FOR BEING HUMAN

1. Use advice like salt. Sparingly.

2. No one's advice is completely objective.

3. We all have some wisdom that we can mine from our experience.

4. If you are taking someone else's advice, do it because you think it's the right thing to do, and not because you're looking to please them or receive validation.

5. While we may have to check our biases, we can still learn to rely on our own judgment.

6. Ultimately, the most important advice is our own.

POSITIVITY, KINDNESS AND THE HUMAN SPIRIT

"You are the sum total of everything you've ever seen,
heard, eaten, smelled, been told, forgot—it's all there.
Everything influences each of us, and because of that
I try to make sure that my experiences are positive."

– Maya Angelou

In my office, we have what we call a "negativity jar." Why? Because work can be challenging, and negative thoughts slip in easily. That client is a jerk. That person is a moron. Whenever we have thoughts that fill the air with bad karma and distract us from moving forward, we deposit money into the jar. That simple contribution reminds us to maintain a positive environment and gets us back on track.

The Law of Attraction has become a guiding principle in my life and is a foundational part of this book. I believe that it contributes to business and personal success, closely intersecting and intertwining with kindness.

The Law of Attraction is the ability to attract into our lives whatever is the target of our focus. Regardless of age, nationality or religious belief, we are all susceptible to the laws that govern the Universe, including the Law of Attraction. The power of the mind translates whatever is in our thoughts and materializes them into reality. In basic terms, all thoughts turn into things, eventually. If you focus on negative doom and gloom you will remain under that cloud. If you focus on positive thoughts and have goals that you aim to achieve, you will find a way to achieve them with massive action.

My friend Maggie taught me a technique that I swear by. I've found it to be a good coping mechanism when dealing with fear and for taking control of my emotions. Whenever I am worried about money, specifically in my business, I stop thinking about it. I let it go and allow a sense of calm to come over me. I assure myself that it will all work out. Every time that I have done this, business has come my way. Every. Single. Time. This is one of the tests I use to remind myself how easy it is to attract good things. Focusing on what you want, but more importantly, releasing the resistance. Positivity alone isn't enough. It's that release—the abolishment of negative thoughts, or the walls that we put up—that's where the magic happens. When you can master this, the goodness flows like a chocolate fountain at a bar mitzvah.

In general, when we indulge our fear, we create a breeding ground for our darkest, most destructive emotions—envy, insecurity, jealousy, suspicion and bitterness. While fear can alert us to danger, dwelling on these associated feelings never leads anywhere constructive. While we need to find outlets to express emotions like these when they come up, it helps if we are able to direct them into something constructive, so that we can ultimately get past them to the more pleasant feelings on the other side.

People are attracted to positivity, and it's contagious. It permeates into every aspect of your day. Even simple exchanges like how you say good morning to your co-workers and spouse or your social media presence. If you complain or bad mouth people, others notice, and it reflects on you. Positive people do better on job interviews and in life in general.

The same goes for kindness. When I first started my company, someone asked me what kind of clients I sought. My answer was succinct: I wanted to work with nice people. To this day, it's still part of our core values.

Kindness can take work. You will often encounter people whom you don't like. Yes, yes, I know this is not breaking news. Trust me, there are a lot of people I don't like. However, understanding how to deal with them is more important to your own peace of mind than it is to theirs. Sometimes, believe it or not, you'll discover that you were wrong about someone, and they end up becoming one of your favorite people. But let's say you really know them and have decided, in no uncertain terms, that they just aren't your cup of tea. How are you going to act? How will you treat them? You know the saying, kill them with kindness? There really is something to that. When you are nice to people, it catches them off guard.

In "Perfect Pairings: The Art of Connecting People," I spend a lot of time talking about connections, the idea that you should strive to make introductions between people—to facilitate life. This, in itself, is an act of kindness.

I challenge you to practice positivity and kindness. Get your own jar. We use ours for charity, but you could use yours for a trip, or student loans, or a personal reward. Or flip it around and reward yourself every time you commit a kind act—create a competition among your friends. Who can fill the jar the fastest? You will find that positivity and kindness can be contagious, so why not create a kindness challenge?

Have An Attitude
Living a more positive life requires a constructive attitude. Don't create problems where they don't exist. Life throws us enough shit—let's not manufacture any extra. In other words, don't be a shit stirrer. Choose to be a conscious student of life. Learn from your mistakes, and make smarter choices as you go along.

Let's say you are a single mom who works three jobs to make ends meet and you stumble across this book. Haha, just kidding. A single mom working three jobs probably wouldn't have time to read this book. I do understand that a positive outlook will not take away all problems. However, it can go a long way toward fending off the kind of despair that makes a difficult situation feel far more hopeless than it really is.

On a practical level, what does this mean? Well, in any given situation, we always get to decide how we'll manage it. We might not be able to make an obstacle vanish, but we can decide whether or not to greet it with determination and a willingness to problem solve, as opposed to giving up, complaining, feeling sorry for ourselves, or reacting with anger.

Like the old saying about lemons and lemonade, you have the options of sitting through life with a sour face, or bringing sweetness to the situation that might well save the day.

Turn that Frown Upside Down

Did you know that smiling is a tool that can make your life better? In "Creating Enchantment," entrepreneur and author Guy Kawasaki talks about smiling as being one of the key components of likeability. And not a fake smile. You want the genuine smile that crinkles up your eyes—the kind of smile that comes from the heart. When you share a smile like that, people can feel your positivity, and they are more likely to want to spend time with you. Although Guy was talking about the importance of an authentic smile as part of building strong business relationships, the mechanics are the same for making personal connections. While the jury is still out on whether or not smiling prevents or causes wrinkles, the more you smile, the less of a bitchy resting face you have. So check one off in the won column.

Upgrade to a Professional

Many people seek the advice and support of a life coach to guide them in making better choices. In fact, life coaching is a huge global industry, estimated at more than a billion dollars! That's because it often does help to get an outside opinion and perspective on your life, especially from someone who does not have a personal, vested interest in your choices.

Whether or not you choose to deal with your problems on your own, with the help of friends and family, or with the guidance of a life coach, therapist/psychiatrist or even a clergyman/woman, the bottom line is that you still have to make a conscious effort to create the type of life you want to live. YOU need to decide to keep a positive attitude. YOU need to decide to be kind to others. YOU need to take responsibility for your choices as you navigate through your days.

The beauty of life is that we get to feel everything. The reality is that you don't get the highs without the lows. That's just the way it is. But again, there are plenty of tools to help you navigate the low points so that you remain open to enjoying the good parts. Even the single mom working three jobs can learn to appreciate precious moments of joy with her kids and find opportunities for laughter and gratitude.

Some Sad Shit

Life IS going to throw us curveballs from time to time. Most of us will face grief at some point. The older we get, the more likely it is that we will lose people who are important to us, or experience some other sort of trauma or tragic loss.

The natural course of life is for children to bury parents, but life doesn't always cooperate with that scenario.

Loss and trauma can strike at times we least expect and alter us forever…and not everyone grieves the same way. I remember talking to a 16-year-old at the funeral of her aunt. She said, "I just don't know how I'm supposed to feel." I knew at that moment she needed comforting advice. I told her that there's no right or wrong answer to handling grief. Everyone processes loss differently. She was relieved to hear that her emotions were perfectly normal.

At the same time, the attitude we adopt in our grief can play a huge role in how we experience our lives. I've been inspired by two women who faced the worst of times with extraordinary attitudes and, as a result, put themselves in strong positions to continue their lives.

My friend Jacqueline's partner of 10 years was shot and killed by an off-duty police officer in a bar fight. His loss left the family in excruciating pain. Acknowledging there is no one way to grieve, Jacqueline has used this as an opportunity to live her life to the fullest, understanding that you never know when today could be your last. She makes no claims of being happy all the time and doesn't pretend her loss never happened. There's no façade. She's transparent about the fact that some of her actions are part of her healing process and may seem unconventional. Regardless, her spirit remains strongly intact. While her heart may never fully recover, the way that she has chosen to exist is admirable.

She travels often and is always up for an adventure. Part of this is to avoid the reality of the world that she is left in without her partner; part is experiencing as much of life as possible. She has moved her career forward by completing a master's degree and getting a new job that allows her the flexibility to travel and enjoy life. She says yes to a lot of things. She's chosen to live the life that her partner Milhouse would want her to. She was only 20 when they met, and he is the only love that she's ever known. She accepts that she may love again, and that it won't be better or worse, just different. She knows that she has many years left on this earth and is confident that she will find someone with whom she is meant to be during this part of her life.

When I think about Jacqueline, I think about the smile on her face—she smiles a lot. She's a firecracker—feisty! She speaks her mind and embraces who she is and what cards have been dealt to her. All she asks is for people to be patient with her on the days where that smile doesn't come as easily.

My cousin Lisa (her real name) lost her husband suddenly, shortly before his 40th birthday. They had two young children, and to say her world was rocked would be an understatement.

But Lisa was blessed with an incredible sense of humor and took this devastating loss in stride. Incredibly transparent about her feelings, she began writing as an outlet. Knowing that her kids counted on her, and that she couldn't afford to hide under the sheets for months, she marched on. Never making excuses or hiding her grief, she made people feel comfortable talking about it. In fact, through her raw and sometimes hilarious storytelling, she discovered that she could help others. She's now completing a book based on her blog and is speaking to young widows and other people dealing with the unexpected loss of a loved one.

Lisa didn't ask to be a young widow and would do anything for her babies to have their daddy back. However, since that is her reality, she made a conscious choice to live fully. She's dealt with her shit gracefully, authentically, and she's found a silver lining in being able to help others. Like Lisa, life can have a quirky sense of humor.

The thing about grief is its unpredictability. There is no time frame for recovering from a traumatic loss. And the cycle of recovery does not travel in a straight line. It goes up and down and all around, and varies over time, even for the same person. My friend Donna lost her husband, who had been quite sick for a long time, so she had more time to prepare than the average person does for losing a spouse. Still, years after his death, she talks about how moments of sadness can well up at unexpected times, after long periods of not really feeling his loss, catching her completely off guard.

For those of you who have lost someone special, it's important to follow your own rhythm for dealing with your grief, and not allow yourself to be told by anyone else how you should be feeling at any given time. Advice like, "You should be over this by now," or "Don't you think it's time to move on," is best ignored. If you have a friend who has lost someone, the most significant thing you can do is just be there for them. Don't try to make it better, or force them to cheer up. Sometimes the hardest thing for someone who is grieving is being alone with their feelings. Being a friendly ear or a shoulder to cry on, without judgment, can be the best way to show you care.

FOMO (Fear of Missing Out)
Another challenging emotional predicament that has probably become more prevalent in the digital age is the fear of missing out, aka FOMO. If you've spent a minute on social media, you

may have observed a friend, family member, or colleague "living the dream." Posts depict them traveling around the world, smiling in every photo, eating at the best restaurants, looking fabulous, and loving life.

Do you really believe that their lives are as perfect as they appear? I'd bet you a pastrami sandwich that they're not. There is more to their stories than meets the eye.

It's true that some people fully embrace the positive side of life. They enjoy each and every moment and share their stories to create a ripple of happiness. I could be accused of that. Rarely do I share the ugly. However, what you see on social media is just a fraction of reality. It's a snapshot of life, not the full-length feature.

Once in awhile, we all fall prey to believing that the grass is greener on the other side…and sometimes it may be! But for the most part, it's really easy to idealize other people's lives and experiences, and focus disproportionately on our perceived deficits and imperfections.

Everyone has a mix of things that give them joy and things that bring them sorrow or frustration, or worse. We'll be most at peace if we can learn to stay centered on our own lives. Sure, we can derive ideas and inspiration from the lives of others, but not to the extent that we forget who we are and what we bring to the table. As much as we can feel like all the action is happening "out there," the truth is that we have the power to bring vitality to our own experiences. There may very well be people out there who are looking at your Facebook pictures thinking, wow, I wish I were where she is right now. In the end, if you feel as though you are always missing out, then maybe it's a sign that you need to be doing more of the things you want to do!

Doing Good

I first began volunteering in high school. I don't even remember why or how I got involved, but I can still feel the warmth in my heart.

My first significant volunteer activity was building a house for Habitat for Humanity. I remember getting up very early on a Saturday morning which, in high school, is no easy feat. I remember feeling empowered as I held a hammer and drove nails into the wall. Seeing the results of my labor was evidence that I had contributed to something important. It felt good. But what I remember most vividly was lunch. I can still taste the creamed corn prepared by the woman who would be living in the house. The food tasted like home. Not my home, but somebody's home. Warm and comforting. The future homeowner had a sense of pride about the meal she served. That pride fueled me as I hammered and painted the walls, knowing that soon the house would be filled with more dishes and memories like the ones created that day.

Twenty-five years later, I remember that time as one of my favorite volunteer experiences, and it kicked off a lifetime of giving back. That satisfaction of helping others produces something called the "Helper's High."[1] Discovered by researcher Allan Luks, this phenomenon, created by the same endorphins that are released when exercising, occurs when helping others. It is incredibly powerful to know that you are working to help somebody else have a better life or get to a better situation.

[1] http://allanluks.com/helpers_high

I'll never forget Cassie, the daughter of one of the shop workers at my company. Cassie had developed a brain tumor that, while not cancerous, had wrapped around her brain, causing paralysis and other terrible challenges. Her father used up most of his sick and vacation time, and both parents were alternating taking time off work to be with her. I was active in the local Kiwanis Club and recruited them to help. We held car washes and placed donation cans all around town to raise money. The entire company got involved, even though none of us had ever met her. Then one day, she was home from the hospital and well enough to come to one of our monthly meetings. She was still in a wheelchair, but was expected to regain more of her mobility soon. She was not really talking, but her smile said everything that her voice did not say. Even as I write this, I smile, knowing we made a difference for Cassie and her family.

I moved shortly after meeting Cassie and tried to start a local Kiwanis Club in my new town, but it never took off. As you know, life gets busy sometimes, and if we are struggling to take care of ourselves, it can be a challenge to take care of others at the same time. I went deep into my business for a long time…and then Hurricane Sandy struck New Jersey.

Most of us remember it well. It hit the night of October 29th, 2012. I woke up on October 30th to no power. It was my birthday, so I went to a friend's house to drink some wine, and by the end of the day, the power returned. However, it did not return for millions of people just a few miles away. A friend contacted me looking for ideas for her brother-in-law, who was among a group of people bringing barbecue to the area to feed people there. She asked if I could help coordinate some locations for them to serve food. I made some phone calls and used social media to connect with some organizations already on the ground. As a result, I developed relationships with some of the other volunteers and those organizations' leaders.

For several years, I helped Operation BBQ Relief by sharing their needs with my network and personally donating financially. Over time, I realized I wanted to be involved at a higher level. I reached out to the group's leadership, and after several conversations, joined their marketing team. For more than a year, I dedicated several hours a day to supporting this organization.

The work was incredibly meaningful. When flooding hit Louisiana in the summer of 2016, I was among the volunteers who traveled there. It was the first time I'd ever experienced a deployment myself. For the most part I'd been helping from the sidelines, behind the scenes, but seeing the devastation firsthand was powerful and affirmed the importance of the work being done.

You might think that after being in the front lines, I got even more involved. Actually, the opposite happened, though not as a result of that trip. Quite simply, the volunteering began to take over my life, and it began to affect the work that paid me and allowed me to make a living. I had to make a tough choice, and that choice was to resign from my position in the organization. Probably the people there took it personally, but it was the right decision for me at the time. I vowed to stay involved and to support the organization through fundraising or anything else it needed. I've done just that, helping to raise several thousand dollars without being in a leadership role.

So what's the moral of the story, you might be wondering? Volunteering is a wonderful thing, but it has to work for you. If it becomes overwhelming, or if it becomes a job, you begin to lose some of those endorphins that it brings. Good volunteers are hard to find, so remember, people will ask as much of you as possible. Setting expectations for yourself and the organization in terms of time and level of commitment helps, but if you find yourself in over your head, don't be afraid to raise a white flag.

There's another, deeper side to volunteering. When we allow ourselves to feel empathy for the suffering of others, we open our hearts to a two-way street of compassion. As any Buddhist will tell you, suffering is an intrinsic part of life. We all go through painful episodes of one type or another during our lives. How we choose to deal with our own struggles will determine a great deal about how we respond to the pain of others. If we allow ourselves to feel victimized by our suffering with thoughts such as, "What have I done to deserve this?" then we are likely to become bitter and angry about the things that happen to us. We are also apt to blame others for their own misfortune, and not feel inclined to help them.

However, if we approach the notion of suffering as a natural part of life and choose to have compassion for ourselves and others for being the vulnerable creatures that we are, we're in a better position to exhibit kindness toward anyone in need. It's hard to compare suffering, as everyone's experience of pain is subjective. But once we accept one another's hardships at face value, we'll be more inclined to respond generously when someone calls out for help.

Now that I've told you all about compassion and empathy, you might think I score high on the empathy scale. The truth is, while I feel empathy intellectually, I am not an overly sensitive person. What I know about compassion is learned. It's part of the reason this book exists. People can become better. If you are reading this and you don't "feel" what you think you are supposed to feel, it's OK. That's all part of being human. Being open to increasing your compassion is a good first step.

That said, engaging in volunteer activities can also bring up uncomfortable realizations about relative privilege or lack thereof, and the underlying injustices that result in these inequities. This is a book topic all on its own, but one point worth making here: If we allow ourselves to see the humanity in one another, it drives us to identify and build on the things we have in common, rather than focus on our differences. When we start from this place, we begin to discover many ways to solve problems, including righting the wrongs of history, in both small and large ways. Volunteering can be an eye-opening experience that inspires us to dig more deeply into making substantial changes in the world around us.

Good things happen to you when you give back. While there may not be a scientific study to prove this, I can attest to the fact that it does come back to you. Helping others is good for your karma, it's good for your soul and it shows you a different side of humanity. If you are thinking about getting involved, find something that engages your passions. I took some time to think about this for myself and decided that feeding people was important to me. I love to eat. I love food, and the fact that there are people who don't have this "luxury" is heartbreaking.

Your passion might be for animals or research or treatment for a specific disease. You might want to do something that involves children or veterans. It doesn't matter, as there is good work to be done everywhere. Kindness comes in all forms, and volunteerism is one of the most rewarding.

LESSONS FOR BEING HUMAN

1. Like attracts like. Positivity attracts positive experiences. Release the resistance and the goodness will flow.

2. Be nice to people. Kindness goes a long way in making the world a better place.

3. Smile more.

4. Grief looks different on everyone. There are no right or wrong responses to loss.

5. Get help when you need it. Don't forget that there are trained professionals out there who can make the process of dealing with challenging emotions less overwhelming.

6. Don't believe everything you see on the internet.

7. Doing good feels good. Give back and you'll be the one who benefits.

WHADDAYA KNOW

"The three great essentials to achieve anything
worthwhile are, first, hard work; second,
stick-to-itiveness; third, common sense."

– Thomas A. Edison

The author Peter Shankman is famous for saying, "In order to be successful you only have to be one level better than crap." Sadly, I've found this to be true—in today's world, mediocrity can get you pretty far. This means that basic success is fairly easy to achieve. The difference between average and that one level above mediocrity can be significant. If you can be two levels above crap, well then you have a pretty bright future ahead of you. A huge factor in leveling up is competence.

I've spent a lot time pondering the concept of competence and how it contributes not just to success, but happiness and contentment. It's not necessarily about any intelligence, but how we manage life's challenges and the opportunities it throws at us. So what exactly is competence? Merriam-Webster Dictionary defines it as "a sufficiency of means for the necessities and conveniences of life." Well, that clarified it for me, how about you?

The easiest way I've found to describe competence is that it is like your internal GPS. It tells you where to go, what to do and helps you navigate right and wrong.

You're reading this book, so I'm gonna assume that you have some intelligence. But are you competent? Competence means so many different things. You can excel in the classroom, but without the ability to navigate the world, you will fail often. I'm really awkward and not very handy. I don't know how to change a tire, but I can certainly get a tire changed. That is competence.

Competence is not necessarily being able to do everything yourself. Rather, it's the ability to get things done in a given situation, whatever needs doing. Whether at school, work or home, competence is knowing how to properly handle the matter at hand. None of us knows everything. Competence extends well beyond knowing how to do things yourself into the territory of understanding the big picture, and knowing who else you need to call on to help you get your mission accomplished.

Sadly, we experience such vast amounts of incompetence in our daily lives that when we see examples of extreme competence, it can be shocking. Here's one: Chewy.com is a company that sells pet products. My cat is overweight and eats only prescription food. Yes, she is high maintenance. One day I placed an order, but I didn't have a chance to send in the prescription. Upon receiving my order, someone from the company called me. Not one of those impersonal robocalls or routine emails. No, it was a real person who took the time to think a few steps ahead, and, predicting the difficulties that might result from unnecessary delays in filling my prescription, who did what she had to do to expedite the process.

What are some things that you can do to be a more competent person? Are you bound by rules and regulations, or the conventions of business as usual? Do you understand how to think on your feet and evaluate when there are extenuating circumstances that may require unique responses? Do you know how to think outside the box? Are you ready to apply lessons you have learned from past experiences?

Think about the most competent people you know. Do you feel safe around them? Confident that they will know how to handle unexpected situations? How can we become more competent within ourselves?

It might seem obvious, but Google is a wonderful place to find information and bring it to the table. If you come to situations prepared with real information, you become a resource and strengthen your ability to add value.

With practice, these things start coming naturally to you. Honesty with yourself about what you know and what you don't know is a critical first step.

Some of the most incompetent people are those who fake it and never admit when they're in over their heads. It's perfectly acceptable to stop and say, I don't know what I'm doing. Asking questions is not a sign of weakness. Au contraire! It's a sign of strength to acknowledge and understand your limitations. It's so much better to raise that white flag earlier in the game, when there is still a chance to turn the situation around. That's a sign of a leader. It will get you much farther in life than faking it until the end and failing. I'm a fan of faking it till you make it, but competence means knowing when to ask for help.

Intuition

Writing this book has been therapeutic for me. It's allowed me to reflect on a lot of my life experiences—the good, the bad and the ugly. You need to learn from life events, even when shitty things happen. And they will continue to happen. The important thing is to see them as opportunities for learning, and not to waste them by not taking a lesson or two away. One huge aspect of this is learning how to trust your intuition—your gut.

What is your gut?

Mary Ellen O'Toole is an FBI profiler and author of the book, *Dangerous Instincts: How Gut Feelings Betray Us*. O'Toole has worked on many high-profile cases, including the Elizabeth Smart abduction and the pursuit of the Unabomber. She describes the gut this way:

"The 'gut' is this nebulous thing somewhere in the body, presumably near the anatomical guts or intestines. Yet no one has ever located this mystical body part, so we can't be sure of its location. The mystical gut cannot be found or measured. We cannot improve it or define it. We can't even compare the accuracy of our gut instincts or feelings to the accuracy of others' gut feelings. We don't know how events and life circumstances impact our gut. We don't know when our gut is having a bad day. Does your gut get better with experience? Is it subject to disease? No one knows. Nonetheless, despite the mystical, magical properties we ascribe to it, many of us assume our gut is among the best, and we rely on it to guide us through life and to help us make life-changing decisions."

Learning how to "trust your gut" is similar to gathering a body of knowledge on a particular topic or learning how to reach out for help when you need it. It's a skill that improves with practice. It's easy to succumb to our insecurities and tempting not to trust our own instincts when the penalty for a wrong choice could leave us regretful or even ashamed. Learning to rely on our collected wisdom is a skill that we hopefully develop with time, evolving alongside the unique life experiences that inform and support it.

Ultimately, when we understand how to combine our learned skills with our innate sensibilities, we end up with something we call common sense. Some would say that common sense is something you're born with, and perhaps some enter into this world with a little more than others. But if you take a little practical knowledge, season it with some intuition, and follow your gut, you will most likely embody the essence of practical sense in everything that you do.

LESSONS FOR BEING HUMAN

1. Don't assume that the person that you're talking to has more or less information than you.

2. Do ask questions.

3. Be transparent about what you know or don't know. It's OK not to have the answers.

4. Do your homework. When in doubt, look it up.

5. Always trust your gut.

THE WORLD AS WE KNOW IT

"All our knowledge is the offspring of our perceptions."

– Leonardo Da Vinci

Today, the United States is riddled with expressions of racism and hatred that I haven't personally seen in my lifetime. I understand that I am most likely exuding white privilege in writing this, and that some of my recommendations in this book are skewed by this perspective. Perhaps we cannot easily change our personal lenses, but we can become more aware of our good fortune and its implications, and practice gratitude. I can share my own shit and embrace it as part of my lens. Most importantly, having an open mind and welcoming diverse views makes us better humans.

In 2015, Coca-Cola released a powerful video before Ramadan. You can watch it at http://bit.ly/PerceptionsVideo. Go ahead and watch, I'll wait.

I've watched this video more than a dozen times, and it gives me chills every time. Spoiler alert if you didn't watch the video: Coca-Cola brings five strangers together in a dark room, where they can't see each other's faces.

They describe their hobbies and interests:	Here are their identifying features. See if you can match them up:
1. Playing heavy metal music	A. Tattoos covering head, face
2. Reading books on cognitive psychology	B. Sits in a wheelchair
3. Studying Arabic culture	C. Conservative gray blazer
4. Cooking	D. Average looking white guy
5. Extreme sports, skydiving	E. Man wearing keffiyeh

If you haven't watched the video, you can take a little quiz to see how you match them up.

Here's the answer key:

1-C; 2-A; 3-D; 4-E; 5-B

If you got them wrong, you are not alone. That's the point of the video, which is called, "Labels are for Cans, Not People." Very clever, Coca-Cola marketing people, very clever.

Like the participants in the video, I would have made a few judgments. This is a very hard thing to overcome. We look at people and situations through our unique filters and apply our personal experience to make interpretations.

A. J. Marsden, PhD is a former U.S. Army surgical nurse who now serves as an assistant professor of human services and psychology at Beacon College in Leesburg, FL, where she teaches a course on theories of personality. I asked Dr. Marsden if there is any science to explain how a person's upbringing and life experience might affect explicit and unconscious bias.

She referenced a 2011 study[2] showing that from a very early age (around six months), babies show a preference for faces of their own race over those of other races, suggesting that we have already developed our in-groups and out-groups before the age of one year. In general, we prefer people, things, places, and events that are comfortable or familiar to us. Thus, when a baby sees something that is vastly different from their norm, they become agitated. Some scientists believe that this suggests that racial bias is hardwired in our brains. However, even though the study shows that babies notice differences in race, it

[2] https://www.ncbi.nlm.nih.gov/pmc/articles/PMC3076379/

does not mean that they will develop negative or positive beliefs about those differences.

Marsden went on to share a meta-analysis [3] showing a significant relationship between parental and child intergroup attitudes:

"It is important to remember that children are little sponges and they soak up more information than we realize. Often, children look to their parents to determine what is right and what is wrong, what is acceptable and what is not, and whom to trust and who to avoid. Furthermore, Patricia Devine, a researcher from the University of Wisconsin [4,5] stated that society, in general, can impact our biases—especially if that society has a history of showing favoritism toward certain groups. Devine called this cultural brainwashing. And despite our conscious efforts to decrease prejudice and racism, people may still internalize their negative attitudes toward minorities."

Marsden's summary of perceptions is eye-opening. It tells us that there may be more at play than we realize when we think about bias. We may, in fact, have to make a concerted effort to overcome our inherent biases. This is the good news and the bad news—bad news because it tells us that we all come to the table with some measure of inherited prejudice. But the good news is that we have the ability to make conscious choices to surpass the limits of our biology! The human brain is complex, but studies like this help us to better understand it and use the information to bring about positive change.

[3] https://www.ncbi.nlm.nih.gov/pubmed/23379964
[4] http://web.comhem.se/u52239948/08/devine89.pdf
[5] http://www.apa.org/monitor/2011/10/biased-brain.aspx

Dr. Marsden continued, "As we gain more and more life experiences, our attitudes further develop, strengthen, or even change. Positive experiences will result in more positive attitudes and negative experiences will result in negative attitudes. However, our brain has a tendency to pay more attention to the negative experiences. Some believe this could be an evolutionary response we developed to keep us safe. Nevertheless, our brains focus more on negative experiences and give more weight to them. Thus, one negative experience could outweigh three positive experiences. Over time, these experiences help us develop schemas, or mental maps, of what will most likely occur in similar situations in the future. For example, let's say you live in Orlando—a city with massive amounts of tourism. Every time you interact with a tourist from New York, they are incredibly rude to you. You will assume that everyone from New York is rude; thus, creating a negative stereotype about that group. In this way, our experiences can shape our biases."

So we know that experiences shape our perceptions, but, as evidenced by the Coca-Cola video, these are not always accurate. So how do we overcome misconceptions to co-exist better? Like many things in life, practice.

Practice taking a step back when you meet somebody or when you encounter a situation that is unfamiliar or uncomfortable. The first step is to try to keep an open mind. Remember, there is some hardwiring involved, so this may be easier said than done. Give it a try anyway. Look at the situation from the opposite perspective or contrary to your instinct, and you may discover a shift in your thinking or come to different conclusions.

Let's say you're working on a project to which you bring a certain point of view, and you believe that this is the right way to do it. Your partner, coworkers or friends disagree. This happens all the time—from school projects to workplace programs to planning your best friend's bridal shower with her overbearing sister and aunt who once had a part-time job in a flower shop and now is an expert.

Regardless of how insignificant the challenge is, put yourself in the other person's shoes. Literally say their words to yourself… "The shower would be fabulous if everyone wore matching pink sundresses and we only served food that starts with the first letter of the bride's name. Zoe is going to have a beautiful day eating zucchini flowers and zeppoles." Come on now, you believe it, right? Did it feel a little better when you said it from another perspective?

We all have our own biases. From planning the perfect bridal shower to managing a major business account to political views, the way you perceive things is not the way that other people perceive them. Even when you think you are on the same page, there are often differences that you just never even thought existed. Navigating these takes patience, good communication and most often, a willingness to compromise.

So, Jessica, are you equating two women quibbling over hors d'oeuvres to heated debates on white supremacy? No. Absolutely not. The former is a simplistic example to show how people think. But the point is still well taken, because we still have to learn to co-exist with people whose views may be radically different from our own, and we still have to contend with the ways our life experience has shaped our perspective on the rest of the world.

Lois educates the public on dealing with people who have certain health concerns. When I first met her, she took a very defensive approach to teaching. She had experienced many negative interactions in the past when approaching people about her own health issues, and she expressed her frustrations during her presentations. More empathetic audiences responded to her style, but others tuned her out. She slowly adapted a more collaborative style—bringing out the pain points of her audience and connecting with them around specific facts rather than appealing to their emotions, in order to bring about a change in their perceptions. When she altered her approach, she became more effective. Not only that, but she became more self-aware of when she became defensive and triggered a warning to herself to change course.

This technique of applying intellectual empathy can be used whenever you are trying to persuade people to look at things from your perspective. Even if there is a good chance that your position is correct, when you see it from the other side, you are better able to support your stance. And putting yourself in the other person's shoes will help to prevent oppositional interactions and offer a pathway to more meaningful discussion.

But what if someone is just an ignorant hardhead? Well, that happens too. Pick and choose your battles, friends. It will preserve your sanity.

Worldly Perspectives

When you think of Nigeria, what comes to mind? Could you find it on a map? Do you imagine it to be a land filled with rich princes who will give you the world if only you send them all of your life savings? Unfortunately for Nigeria, a handful of scammers have created a very bad perception of the country.

Over the last few years I have become friends with two people who live in Nigeria.

I first heard Olanike Oluboji speak at Mashable's Social Good Conference. She calls herself a passionate gender and environmental advocate. From the moment I encountered her, I was mesmerized. She has dedicated her life to making the world and environment a better place. She raises awareness for issues affecting women, such as the toxic effects of wood-burning stoves. After the conference, I reached out to her to tell her I was inspired. She wrote me back a message that now hangs in my office. It reads…"Together, we can change the world."

Over time, we began to exchange messages, and on occasion we'd Skype, but electricity and internet is scarce where she lives. Then I learned she would be in New York for a program. Serendipitously, her cousin lives in my town, a five minute drive away. I invited her for dinner. I served some wine and cheese and snacks. Her tastes were simple, and she enjoyed the almonds the best. This alone was significant, as I wanted to impress her and didn't take into account her preferences or previous exposure to certain cuisine. I also made a poor assumption that she enjoyed wine as much as I do. Nevertheless, we had a wonderful visit. She brought me a handmade hat from one of the women in her community. I bought five more for my friends.

44

She talked to me about her life—about the many jobs she held, and the challenges she faced getting to work safely and then, once she was there, how she was harassed by the men she worked with. Yet, despite the shit she has had to deal with, she is unstoppable. She shared that her dream is to win a Nobel Prize for her environmental work. If anyone has a chance, it's Olanike. Our process of getting to know one another opened my eyes to our differences, even as we discovered the things we had in common.

Around the same time, I was contacted to speak at a conference in Lagos, Nigeria. Yes, my initial impression was that it was a scam, but I agreed to take a call with the planner. His name was Ofuma, and he made me understand that it was a legitimate opportunity, even going so far as to put me in touch with former speakers to reassure me that the conference was real. He had reached out to me because he needed a marketing speaker, and Nigeria lacked marketing experts. During our discovery conversations, I realized that Ofuma himself was knowledgeable on the topic. He read all of the industry publications and had done his homework. He understood my concerns as we discussed travel plans, security, etc.

Encouraged by Ofuma's transparent and informed communication, I took the first steps to overcome my initial skepticism, and we developed the foundation for an ongoing connection with one another.

For various reasons, the conference never came to fruition, but Ofuma and I began a friendship. We discussed marketing techniques and entrepreneurship. We became connected on Facebook, which gave me insight into how his local friends and family viewed him. Our trust in one another deepened.

Both Olanike and Ofuma have remained my friends. Olanike visits whenever she is in town. Ofuma and I regularly exchange ideas about business and life. I feel fortunate that they entered my world and broadened my views. Everyone should have people like them in their lives. People who shift your thinking and make you realize we are all just humans trying to exist.

One of the things that I've found to be most transformational, in terms of my own perspective on the world, is travel. When you travel, you experience different cultures and ways of life. In the United States, the East and West coasts tend to be more culturally diverse, and the people who live there tend to be more liberal. You can look at any map of political preferences to see that blue states tend to be located on the coasts. This is no accident! When you have people interacting with and getting to know others who are significantly different from themselves, you end up with a wider perspective all around. Prejudice is often born of ignorance and lack of exposure.

If you've never known somebody with a different skin color who practices a different religion from you, you may have preconceived notions of who they are. It's only when you get to meet them that these opinions can fade away, as you get to experience the actual person, instead of some imaginary scenario made up in your head.

When you travel, you see places, traditions and people that may be very different from your own upbringing, but if you look closely you might just find unexpected commonalities. You might realize that the scenarios that you conjured up are not accurate at all, and that people who live on the other side of the country or even on the other side of the world, who believe different things from you, might be more similar to you and others like you than you thought.

Christine is the founder of Wunderbar Travel, which is dedicated to cruise vacations. Her parents were both born and raised in Soviet-occupied East Germany, and she spent her childhood living behind the Berlin Wall. Living isolated in a socialist state their whole lives, the family didn't know anything different from what they personally experienced.

Once the entire country collapsed and everything changed (from banking to insurance, house rental prices, and how things were done in general) her parents found themselves at a loss. It seemed that everything they knew and everything they had become was somewhat worthless, and they had to start from scratch in a new country.

Christine's family's journey shaped her views of the world in interesting and powerful ways. She learned that possessions are not very important. While living in East Germany, her family had means to travel within the territory. However, even though they were enjoying a new type of freedom after the wall came down, and could travel wherever they wanted to go, they suddenly didn't have the money to make those trips. Instead of expensive vacations, they spent holidays at her grandparents' place near the Baltic Sea. Quality time was valued, and her parents spent time with the kids every weekend. They window-shopped at toy stores "just to look," but never buy.

"The hard times taught me that possessing things doesn't make you necessarily happier. I would see trends among kids and wasn't able to have those things myself, but three months later when the fad had passed, it wasn't much of an issue anymore.

The lesson here for me is that now I ask myself every time that I am about to buy something, if the purchase is really necessary and whether it will really make me happier. In most of the cases the answer is 'No,' and so I leave it in the store."

Christine tells a story that put things in perspective. It hit me hard, as she spent an internship working in a place that I have dreamed of visiting, The Seychelles.

"When I worked in The Seychelles, they had to import nearly everything from Dubai and Mauritius. For example, it could take up to six weeks to receive a delivery of yoghurt. At this point, you'd better like pineapple yoghurt or whatever flavour they would ship that month—because there was nothing else to buy. After a while, I realized that most citizens of the Seychelles didn't even shop in the expensive import supermarket. They had smaller supermarkets that were mainly run by people from India, who sold exactly one brand of each everyday item. One brand of toilet paper, one brand of chocolate, one brand of jam, one brand of dishwashing liquid. After my discovery, I started buying at the local shoppe and didn't notice a difference. Spending less on staple items, I instead enjoyed the natural beauty of the island and the scuba diving.

"During the internship I made a whopping $400 a month (but had free accommodation), and I became friends with the locals... I finally started to trust the people over there and get rid of this 'everybody is trying to scam you' attitude."

By actually getting to know the people, Christine became more trusting. It's funny how that happens. People are largely abstract until we attach a name, face and other details to the person. Then, they become human to us.

"I think a lot of people that we meet around the world are a lot nicer than we expect them to be, and not everybody is out there to scam tourists and to take things from them. Once I started to let my guard down a little bit, I felt that I had a better time in general.

"During my travels, I ended up with Egyptians in the desert around Cairo, riding on horseback in the middle of the night and drinking tea before returning back to the city center. I think that must have been one of the craziest things I've ever done, and when I tell the story, people ask me whether I wasn't scared that somebody would kidnap me. I wasn't, because I felt that the people that I was with were genuine. When we were in Rio de Janeiro, I walked around on my own, and the people in Ho Chi Minh City were incredibly nice to me as well. I just think as long as one doesn't act entirely stupid and keeps the jewelry at home and smiles at people and is friendly, one can have amazing experiences. My goal is now to see as many countries and places around the world as I can."

Brava, Christine. I hope you make those travel dreams a reality.

LESSONS FOR BEING HUMAN

1. Question your assumptions about people. You may be operating from biases you don't even realize you have.

2. We are born with a genetic affinity for people who look like us, but we can grow beyond that.

3. Our brains are hardwired to remember negative experiences to protect us from danger, but those experiences don't have to define us.

4. Over time, life helps us grow beyond our inherited tendencies and early perceptions, so allow yourself to evolve.

5. Get out and see the world! The more different kinds of people you meet, the more your perspective widens.

NO ONE'S PERFECT

"Life is not easy for any of us. But what of that?
We must have perseverance and above all confidence
in ourselves. We must believe that we are gifted for
something, and that this thing, at whatever cost,
must be attained."

– Marie Curie

Professor Robert Plomin of the Institute of Psychiatry, King's College, London, and his colleague Corina Greven have conducted research[6] showing that children's self-perceptions of their abilities have a clear genetic basis. Their team asked more than 3,700 twin pairs to rate their abilities in a number of core school subjects. By studying both identical and non-identical twins, from the age of seven to ten, they were able to assess the relative contributions of genes and environment.

Contrary to accepted wisdom, they found that confidence is heavily influenced by genetics.

"Everyone has assumed self-confidence is a matter of environment. Our research shows that it is certainly genetically influenced and that self-confidence predicts achievement at school." Professor Plomin added: "We are not saying that genes are the only factor or that upbringing and environment cannot change things. But there is something genetic in self-confidence which I would think of as a personality trait that would be stable throughout life."

On one hand, our DNA is partly responsible for confidence, but there is more to it. Our brain chemistry, which is fluid, also shapes confidence. Keisha Blair, co-founder of Aspire-Canada, an online platform for young professionals, studies confidence through her practice developing policies for clinical social workers helping kids in the social welfare system. Blair shares, "Neuroreceptors in the brain responsible for confidence are linked to dopamine. These receptors are more developed in some individuals than in others. Men also seem to have an advantage over women, because they have approximately 52

---

[6] http://journals.sagepub.com/doi/pdf/10.1111/j.1467-9280.2009.02366.x

percent more serotonin[7] than women and have much more testosterone levels in their bodies. Studies also show that when men's testosterone levels drop they take less risks than men with very high levels of testosterone[8]."

Dr. A. J. Marsden also notes that there are many factors that influence confidence. "It starts in childhood with parents' attitudes toward their children. When parents are accepting, encouraging and understanding, it builds a child's confidence. If, however, they are overprotective or discourage independence in the child, it can negatively affect their confidence. The child may start to feel incapable or inadequate. Parents who allow their child to try something and fail do more for that child's confidence than if parents keep their child from failing. [Helicopter parents take note!]

"Friends and peers can also influence confidence. Friends who support you and celebrate your accomplishments will help build your confidence more than peers who do not. When friends, peers, or parents criticize what you do or how you do something, it becomes a significant challenge to develop any confidence."

So it seems that confidence is borne of a mix of genetic predisposition, experience that affects our brain chemistry, and direct feedback from the people in our lives, that affects our overall attitude toward ourselves.

I really wanted to know more about how the concept of failure fit into all of this. Dr. Marsden weighed in again, explaining,

---

[7] https://www.ncbi.nlm.nih.gov/pmc/articles/PMC24674/
[8] http://www.open.edu/openlearn/science-maths-technology/science/biology/how-testosterone-affects-risk-taking-behaviour

"Failures can be very beneficial in building confidence—depending on how you handle the failure."

Wanting to test Dr. Marsden's theory on someone with proven success, I spoke to Australian freestyle skier and Olympic champion Lydia Lassila, who took home a gold medal at the 2010 Winter Olympic Games in Vancouver and a bronze in Sochi in 2014. As she prepares to compete in 2018, I asked her about how failure contributes to her confidence, as she flies through the air and manages to land on her feet. Yes, I know, asking an athlete about failure as they are getting ready for the world stage isn't super motivating, but I suspected she would have some insight. You see in 2006, during the second qualifying round of the Torino aerials competition, Lassila's knee collapsed on impact after she attempted to land a difficult jump, re-rupturing a previous injury in her ACL and forcing her to withdraw from the Olympic Games. She said, "I certainly have had many failures, and I don't think I would have learned as much about myself or what I'm capable of without them. Preserving confidence is a constant battle...the failures seem to eat away at it, but problem solving them and figuring out how you can be/do better and overcoming them is what restores confidence."

Clearly, a number of factors come into play in determining a person's confidence level, but an individual's environment still plays a big role, as it stems from how one is raised and begins from one's earliest memories. I was very fortunate to have a grandmother, Nana Joyce, and great-grandmother, Nana Francie, who told me I was pretty. All. The. Time. Nana Francie also mentioned, every time I saw her, that I would be the first woman president and as a result of her certitude, I grew up believing that anything is possible. It was only during the 2016 election, 17 years after her death, that I realized how profound this was as I watched women flock to the gravesite of Susan B. Anthony on election day to place their "I voted" sticker on her tombstone. At that moment, it clicked that my great-grandmother was born 14 years before women had the right to vote in the United States. And even though she grew up at a time where women usually stayed home and raised babies, she saw different opportunities for me. Her assurance that I could do whatever I wanted translated into my own confidence throughout my whole life. I am pretty certain that had she been born a few decades later, she would have been an entrepreneur, like I am today.

But there's a flipside to the praise. Since I was eight, I have struggled with my weight. While Nana Joyce often complimented my face, there was rarely ever a time when she didn't remind me to "watch what I eat." In fact, several days before she died, I was on the phone with my grandfather discussing my upcoming back surgery. In the background she said, "Could it be because of her weight?" relating to why I needed surgery. Those were the last words I ever heard her say. The very last words! Like that wasn't going to cause any psychological damage to me.

Even with the best intentions, confidence building can be very complicated.

Many people who appear to be confident actually lack self-esteem. These people have just gotten really good at masking their insecurity, and it often comes across through aggression and intimidation. They may try to make others feel bad about themselves as a defense mechanism.

This chapter is designed to help you get a handle on your own confidence and to understand the complex factors that influence it. Building your confidence by loving yourself first and embracing both your good and bad qualities leads to a life of opportunity and success. Accepting that we are not perfect, and that, yes, we all have faults is empowering. Confidence helps you identify areas for self-improvement without anger or resentment.

Confidence is something that I've spent a lot of time thinking about, especially as a business owner. I've spent a lot of my career working with men who were older than I, and as a woman, even in 2017, you have to have a lot of confidence to do that. Some of that comes naturally to me—it's ingrained in my DNA. But I know that some of it takes work and some comes with maturity. I am much more confident today than I was the day I graduated college, and I'm sure that I'll be much more confident 10 years from now. It's something I continue to pay attention to, because I know it factors into success. Whether it's natural to you or not, don't worry, it will improve over time.

If you are struggling a bit with your own confidence, take note. The truth is, most people are too busy thinking about themselves to think about you or to laugh at you or to make fun of you—they are too busy being insecure themselves to worry about you. If you go with that, you're already one step ahead of the game.

If you are still concerned, consider this. Generally, people assume that you know what you're doing, so as long as you act like it, in whatever situation you're in, you should be okay. How's that for a load off your mind?

It's a funny thing, talking about one's own confidence. I have received many accolades in my professional life, and I walk a balancing line between being proud of those and not being arrogant. I've only recently learned to accept a compliment and simply say thank you without making excuses for my achievement. I don't like to brag, and believe there's a time and place to acknowledge accomplishments. Be appreciative and grateful for what you have achieved and for the people who have supported you along the way.

One more important part of being confident is your ability to admit mistakes. When you are wrong, say so. Humility is honesty, and signals to others that you are ready to engage and to learn new things. It indicates an openness and a willingness to grow that makes you a good collaborator, a valuable skill in today's marketplace. On the personal side, it also shows that you have what it takes to be a good friend and life partner. Who wants to engage with someone who's always right, or at least thinks they are?

When looking at other people, don't mistake strong personalities for strong people. Confidence is easy to fake. The tougher people seem, the more vulnerable they probably are. Truly strong and confident people are not afraid to be vulnerable. They are not afraid to be wrong.

Of course, just as with most things, there is a fine line between confidence and overconfidence. Overconfidence can be seen as arrogance. Hint: If you are concerned with being arrogant, you're probably not a jerk.

Wonder Woman embodies all that is confidence. Okay, yeah, she's a beautiful demigod with magical powers. She's also strong and compassionate. She commands respect because she is free from self-doubt, yet feels the plight of others. She owns her role in the world and doesn't make excuses for who she is. She stands tall and proud and doesn't care what other people think about her. Don't you just adore Wonder Woman?

Sexy Underwear

Fear of public speaking, or glossophobia, ranks among the top of many people's dreads. For some people it's absolutely terrifying. For me, it's one of the most exhilarating things in the world. I often joke that I wanted to be an actress, more specifically a "movie star," when I was little, and since that didn't pan out, I became a public speaker. People are baffled by the fact that I rarely get nervous before I speak, and on those few occasions when I do, I tend to perform better and have the best presentations.

People have asked my advice about how not to be nervous before speaking in front of others. My friend Jane is more terrified of presenting than I am of snakes. And I'm really, really scared of snakes. One day Jane was asked to give a very brief presentation at her company about her job. All she had to do was talk about who she was, her experience of the company and what her job entailed. Easy peasy, right? Jane built up so much anxiety about this presentation, she wasn't sleeping at night. So when she asked me to help her conquer her worst fear, I gave her my best trick in the book. Wear sexy underwear!

This might be TMI, but whenever I present, I wear my best and sexiest underwear, usually a matching bra and panty set. I give presentations about straight business things like marketing and technology, so it's not like I'm doing a striptease, right? This has nothing to do with what people see, but it has everything to do with how I feel. When I wear sexy underwear, I feel more confident. I feel more put together, and I know something that the audience doesn't know. It's that simple.

OK, OK, there is something else, too. The audience assumes that you know your subject matter and are going to teach them something that they don't know. It's the reason you are up front taking the stage and sharing your information. For the most part, they are not mocking you. They are not laughing. They might not even be thinking about you at all. Why? Because everyone is dealing with their own shit. Hopefully you're holding their attention and saying something of value, and they're listening to the content of your presentation. But if they're not, it is more likely that they are thinking about having to pick up the kids from school or do the laundry or the fight they just had with their spouse. If we are being really honest, they're probably thinking about the make-up sex. They're probably not judging you, because you are at the front of the room, and you have the perceived authority about whatever subject you're talking about. And do you really care if somebody else is judging? As long as your boss isn't unhappy and ready to fire you, it doesn't really matter what they think.

My friend ended up getting through her presentation without vomiting. I call that a win.

Some people's weaknesses are others' strengths. Jane would rather have a root canal than speak in front of a crowd, but she owns it at the gym. We work out together, and after five minutes I'm wiped, and she can go full force for hours. She probably wasn't the very last person to get picked for the kickball team in grade school and wasn't traumatized for life during dodgeball like her workout buddy, so who cares if she pees her pants before presenting?

There are some exceptions to this rule. I get paid to speak and am subject to session evaluations. The comments can be pretty harsh. I've read comments about my physical appearance, about my clothes, about how I talk with my hands, etc. Once I was rated one of the top speakers in the whole conference. Yay me, right? I received lots of "absolutely fantastics" and "awesomes." Then there was, "She has an attitude." During the wrap-up with my client, he shared this comment with me, and he said, "Yes, you do. That's exactly why we hired you." So whether you have to present at work or in front of the PTA or you really do want to be a public speaker, go out, buy the sexiest pair of underwear you can find and rock it.

Heavy Stuff

I've lost and gained hundreds of pounds over my lifetime and, on several occasions, took off quite a bit of weight all at once. For the most part, from an emotional perspective, I did not hate carrying extra weight, but other people certainly had opinions about my body.

Nana loved to throw around the word, "heavy." At her funeral, during my eulogy, I promised her that I would "do something about it." Those were her words. She always wanted me to "do something about it." But when I finally decided to focus on real and permanent weight loss, it was not because of how I looked but because of how I felt. I felt like crap—my whole body hurt, and I was taking bottles of medicine every day. I simply was not healthy and admitted that I needed professional help, as I could not do it alone.

Realizing that I needed support was empowering. Admitting you need help is not easy to do, but once you do it, everything can change. I began to share my weight loss journey publicly and was proud to have finally gotten a handle on my health issues. This is where some of the real lessons appeared, especially as I started sharing photos of my body transforming. Not like a mythological shapeshifter, although some days it felt that way.

I admit I can be vain, and felt I was looking pretty hot. I had always felt sexy, there was just a little more of me to love...I'm a girl who likes a good compliment, and appreciates the kind words and support of friends who encourage me to stick with it.

I do not ever want to feel ungrateful, but there are nuances to this. When people start to tell you how good you look now, it becomes apparent how bad they thought you looked before. Here I am, living my life, trying to be a good person and all the time I have friends and family thinking, "Wow, Jessica's great...if only she wasn't such a heifer."

Am I being overly sensitive? I don't think so. I've been told straight out that I was fat by people I thought were on my team. I am so appreciative of my cheerleaders who are proud of me, but not everyone is sincere or baggage-free in their communications.

One day I received a text message from a longtime friend who had a history of building me up after she put me down. After seeing that I had lost weight, she sent me a message telling me that I looked very happy, and she was glad that I was no longer hiding behind a facade. A facade? Really? I never felt like I was hiding from anything. And who was she to say that? During a previous attempt at weight loss, she remarked that she knew that there was always a thin person hiding inside of me just waiting to come out. A whole thin person in me? I mean I did lose ¼ of my body weight, but a whole other person? This is mind boggling. That thin person must have been hiding behind my internal organs or something magical. Or did she mean my soul? Did you know that souls can be fat or skinny? I certainly didn't.

Not surprisingly, I had to re-evaluate this relationship, as this was part of a larger pattern of her projecting things onto me that didn't seem to be mine. Her shit involved growing up with an abusive father and being in abusive relationships. As a result, she abused others as part of the vicious cycle she was caught in. I decided that, while I understood where her shit stemmed from, that it was not healthy for me to be treated poorly by her. I backed away from the friendship.

She wasn't the only one to suggest that I was happier with a lower number on the scale. I was, in fact, happier, but that stemmed from feeling better not necessarily wearing a small size.

You'll never fully understand what is happening inside someone—why they are making the changes they are making, and why they feel the way they do after the changes take place. There was a time when I had physical pain every day for more years than I can remember, and when I changed my diet, this pain went away. I recently began a vegan diet, because I was suffering from extreme inflammation in my body and discovered that a modified diet could help manage the pain. After a couple of months, I began to feel better and yes, the scale moved. I took photos of myself, and of course, I looked thinner and my skin definitely had a different glow to it. I believe this was a direct result of eating actual nutrition rather than pizza five days a week…okay I'm exaggerating, only three days a week.

So yes, absolutely, the change in diet made me happy, but many people missed the point by assuming that my happiness came from weight-loss and from not being fat. Actually, I was just thrilled to not be in pain.

When you comment on someone's physical appearance, even if you mean well, it's risky territory. Unless you know that it's completely appropriate and welcome, don't say anything. If you are going to offer commentary, keep it positive and don't reference their former or their future appearance. Don't talk about their goals unless they invite you to do so. Don't say things like, "If you only lose a few more pounds, you'll be there." It's hard enough for people to deal with their own demons, they don't need yours as well. If you want to extend a compliment, remark about how giving they are, how they always make you feel special. Congratulate them on a work success or on winning a softball game. Humans do great things. Celebrate them for it.

This notion might be best summarized by Al Roker of *Today Show* fame who said, "People who are overweight don't want unsolicited advice. Guess what. We know we are fat. We live in homes with mirrors." Touché, Mr. Roker. Touché.

And one last piece of advice when it comes to comments. Unless you are 777% certain that a woman is pregnant and you know her well, DO NOT ask her about it. Don't try and touch her belly. Just don't go there.

Mental Illness

After 30 years of struggling with my weight, feeling like I was a failure over and over again, I finally found a doctor who officially gave me a diagnosis. I have binge eating disorder. Yay! Most people wouldn't be excited to be diagnosed with a disease. However, when you feel like for most of your life there's been something wrong with you that you could not explain, being officially diagnosed brings a sense of relief.

Prescription medicine now treats my addiction, and while it's effective in some ways, this is still a daily struggle. For someone who has never suffered from addiction, it can be hard to comprehend. Basically, I rationally and logically understand that I should not be eating certain foods. I know I should not eat leftover holiday desserts that are sitting in my fridge. The intellectual in me understands this; I'm an intelligent person. However my brain does not always agree with itself, and there is a stronger force at work causing me to eat, even when I know I shouldn't. It can be very difficult for somebody with normal brain chemistry to understand a brain that doesn't function properly. Unlike an alcohol or nicotine addiction, our bodies require food and simply not eating isn't an option. This makes it particularly challenging to live with in a society in which food is celebrated and is often the center of social events and family gatherings.

You might be surprised to learn that when I think about my own eating disorder, I am grateful. My heart is full of gratitude that I can afford to feed myself. The irony is not lost on me, that I cannot stop eating while many people wish they had one solid meal a day. But unfortunately, as anybody who has suffered from binge eating and who can afford at least one meal a day understands, knowing that many suffer from starvation is not enough to curb your appetite.

Depression is another of life's difficulties. I can speak to this, because over the course of my life I've suffered at times from mild depression. Fortunately, I have overcome those episodes through positive thinking, therapy and exercise. Those tools alone have allowed me to emerge from a state of depression and resume a normal and prosperous life. Not everyone is as lucky. Depression and bipolar disorder are very real and serious medical conditions. People who suffer from these disorders cannot control the way they feel. It's not as simple as reading this book and flipping a switch, so that all of a sudden they're able to lead a positive and happy life.

It's important to note that while I believe many people can practice positivity and kindness, this can be a real struggle for someone whose brain just won't cooperate. If you or someone you know struggles with depression, reading this book won't necessarily fix that. But what you might be able to do is absorb this information and process it in a way that works for you. Leading a better life isn't all or nothing. Take the wins that come to you and be thankful when they do.

Humans are far from perfect, and it's easy to get caught up in our shit. Owning who we are takes practice. It takes work. Improve every day, but give yourself permission to embrace who you are at this given moment.

And when in doubt, place your hands on your hips, stand up straight and channel your inner superhero. If you need it, throw on a cape, too, and take on whatever comes at you, like you've got super powers.

LESSONS FOR BEING HUMAN

1. Confidence is a strange brew of nature and nurture. With the right support and determination, you can always become more confident!

2. Don't be afraid to fail—overcoming failure might be your ticket to success.

3. Humility also goes a long way in helping you grow and nurture a strong sense of self.

4. When in doubt, wear sexy underwear.

5. Honestly, everyone's worried about themselves, so you can relax more than you think.

6. Don't comment on a woman's pregnancy unless you know for sure she's pregnant. Trust me on this one.

7. People will have lots to say about how you should be. Follow your own path and only accept advice when you really ask for it and believe it's right for you.

RELATIONSHIPS

"Truth is everybody is going to hurt you:
you just gotta find the ones worth suffering for."

– Bob Marley

Aaaah, relationships. This is one of those topics that could take up a whole book, let alone a chapter. We're social creatures after all, and we need other people in our lives. Hopefully, as you go through life, you develop friendships that will stand the test of time. You may find romantic partners who also commit to be with you for the long term. But modern life has gotten so complex. The different options we have for interacting with one another continue to multiply and evolve so quickly, it's hard to keep up with the changing social landscape. Ultimately, I'm an optimist when it comes to dealing with people, but there are some significant challenges that can come up that are worth exploring in more detail.

Save the Drama for Your Mama

Introvert, extrovert, or anything in between, we have all had days where we feel like hiding under the covers or moving to a deserted island so that we don't have to deal with other people. As we get older, we tend to increase our understanding of just how complicated people are, but also have less tolerance for BS. While "Grumpy Old Man Syndrome" can be a medical condition resulting from low testosterone, it can also simply be a decrease in one's ability to deal with other people's shit.

Do you have anyone in your life who makes you feel like there's always drama? Perhaps they always have something mean to say. Or maybe they borrow money, promise to pay it back and never do. Some people have a strong sense of loyalty through good times and bad. I get it. I'm super loyal and a really good friend. However, people who take advantage of you, people who are mean to you, are toxic. And you don't need toxic in your life. Just because someone is dealing with their own shit, you don't have to be part of that shit.

You can give yourself permission to be free.

Don't stop talking to your best friend over a petty fight. Disagreements happen, and that's not what I'm talking about. This is about identifying people who suck the life out of you—negative people who can't get out of their own way, no matter how much support you give them. People who blame others for their shit and never take responsibility. Those people are toxic, and sometimes we bring toxic people into our lives without even realizing it.

So how do you determine whether someone's presence is so negative that it's time to cut that person out of your life? The answer is different for everyone. I had a tumultuous relationship with my father and attempted to make things work for many years. I'll spare you the details. Despite his pattern of selfish behavior, I made an effort to have a relationship with him. The tipping point came when my sister needed him and he refused to be there. She was 18 and needed a place to live. At 25, I was not in any position to support her and begged our father to provide a home for his daughter. His response stung my soul. He said, without emotion, that he was not going to get another divorce over one of his children. That was my breaking point. After all the years of neglect, of him missing happy occasions in my life, the final straw was when he hurt someone else whom I loved dearly. This was evidence that he was the problem, and I made a decision that I did not want that in my life.

This was a difficult story to share but worth it. My life today is rich, and I've filled it with many surrogates who offer support and encouragement in a way that feels caring and nurturing.

There are times, like on Father's Day, where I feel sad about not having my father in my life. However, on most days I am free of the hurt that he caused and the potential for further pain.

This is freeing and comforting, and confirms for me that in the end, I made the right choice.

The decision to end a relationship shouldn't be taken lightly. It's not a resolution that should be made reactively, as some sort of punishment. Rather, it should be a proactive choice, made in your own best interests, after careful thought and consideration of all the ramifications. Truly ending a relationship means more than just unfriending someone on Facebook. You'd better be sure of what you are choosing to do, because in most cases, there's no going back.

Getting rid of toxic people (seriously—get rid of them) feels like a huge weight lifted off of your shoulders. There is a difference between being a loyal friend and a patsy who holds on to someone who is toxic. It takes time to learn when to let go, but when you do, it makes all the difference. And when you do realize who your core crew is—embrace them like there's no tomorrow.

Family Defined
Years ago I read about Hawaiian culture and "ohana," which means extended family, including cousins, neighbors and friends. I loved everything about the concept and emulate it in my life. Sometimes our chosen family can be among the nearest and dearest people to us. I have met people on Twitter who now sit at my Thanksgiving table. Over time we have created our own holiday traditions, blending long-established practices with our own spin.

Your support system is one of the most important keys to success and overall happiness. If you come from a solid birth family, appreciate and honor them. But, if for any reason you don't have a close family, even if it's just due to proximity, don't be afraid to build your own ohana. You don't have to run out and find a partner and pop out babies to fill the void. Build a community around you of people who will hold you up and love you for who you are. Don't be afraid to define who is in your life and who isn't.

My Christmakah dinner is always open to 'holiday orphans' and we've made the best memories. There's always room for one more at the table.

Give Fewer Fucks
One of my favorite authors, Mark Manson, wrote a 2013 article titled, "Fuck Yes or No." The basic premise is that whether it's a romantic or personal relationship, if the person is not a fuck yes then they are a no. I've read and shared this article countless times and it has changed my life. Manson recently published a book, "The Subtle Art of Not Giving a F*ck," which gave me pause. In it, he explains that you really have to figure out what you give a fuck about, stop caring about trivial things and focus on what matters. A big part of this is not caring what other people think about you.

During a recent night out with some friends, we were discussing age and wisdom. The women were all in their 40s or turning 50. The common thread among the group was that as you age, you care less and less what other people think. You speak your mind more and essentially give fewer fucks. As you age, you own your shit more.

Owning your shit and giving fewer fucks is not an excuse to be an asshole. (Sorry, couldn't resist crafting such a profane sentence.) You should be kind to everyone, especially to those people about whom you don't give a fuck. When you are kind to other people, even those who treat you terribly, don't respect you or are just plain idiots, your kindness is not about them. Being kind is about you. You cannot control how other people think or act. Sure, you can try to influence them, and by being positive and kind, it may rub off on them, but that's not your responsibility. Your responsibility is to be the best person that you can be. Be kind, so that when you go to bed at night you know you did, as my Nana would say, the right thing.

Fuck Yes or No
It's OK to say No. And Yes.

I have had periods in my life where I have intentionally made an effort to say yes. Yes to adventures. Yes to opportunity. Yes to a challenge that pushed me outside my comfort zone. Saying yes is empowering, because you open yourself up to new experiences—to potentially life-changing memories.

If you're a person who is used to saying no, saying yes can move you to a whole new dimension. However if you are a person who is used to saying yes all the time, you may discover and already know, that life can get overwhelming very quickly.

One of my favorite sayings is, "If you want to get something done, ask a busy person." There are a lot of reasons why somebody might be a yes person.

Sometimes it's ambition, sometimes it's that they don't want to let people down. And sometimes, yes people hit their limit and realize that they have to start saying no.

I've gone through times when I never said no. The problem is that when you overcommit, you don't do anything well. I've found myself becoming resentful of things that at one time brought me a lot of joy. Organizations that I had been a part of for many years, to which I had given my heart and soul, things I really loved, all of a sudden became a burden, and there was no joy. That's when I made a decision to start saying no. I'd love to tell you that this all worked out like in Lifetime movies. But, no, this is reality TV. People were disappointed in me. People stopped talking to me and made me feel like I'd let them down.

Emotions aside, I had neglected parts of my business, and it affected my income. I'd certainly neglected my health, and my stress was at an all-time high. Once I started saying no, it became so much easier to continue. And that gave me an opportunity to regroup and help in smaller though still significant ways. Instead of spreading myself thin, I was able to make more meaningful contributions to the world. Sometimes by saying no you are really saying yes.

If you are looking to bring more balance to the yes-and-no in your life, here are some activities and commitments to consider, in re-thinking your responses:

- Volunteering in professional organizations
- Taking a leadership role in your community civic or religious organization
- Babysitting your friend's or family's children

- Going out on a Friday night after you've had a long week
- Going out in the middle of the week
- Lending someone money
- Sex
- Going on a roller coaster
- Taking a trip
- Running a marathon

Just think. When presented with the opportunity to do any of these things, you have the option to say yes or no. It's up to you how and with whom you spend your time. The freedom is almost dizzying, isn't it?

LESSONS FOR BEING HUMAN

1. Don't keep toxic people in your life. It's not worth it.

2. You can create your own, loving version of an extended family.

3. Own your shit and give fewer fucks, but don't be an asshole. Seriously.

4. Don't forget that you have the power to say yes and no whenever you choose.

5. Practice keeping good boundaries—it's an essential survival skill.

LOVE IS A DRUG

"Tis better to have loved and lost
than never to have loved at all."

– Alfred Lord Tennyson

If ever there was a subject that deserved a chapter all to itself, this is it. Falling in love is one of the most amazing experiences in the world. It can be magical, ethereal, transformational. It can elevate your experience of everyday life to unimagined heights of joy, turn the most mundane activities into moments of sublime pleasure. Falling in love is the stuff of ballads and ballets, poetry and plays. If you are lucky enough to be in love, then my one piece of advice to you is, relax and enjoy it…because the flip side can be a real bear.

Have you ever had a broken heart? If not, congratulations. Most people have gone through this experience at some time in their lives. And yes, a broken heart is a real thing. That pain you feel is not just in your head. There are real chemical reactions that take place when you fall in love and when you experience a break-up.

I'm the type of person who falls in love hard. Given the fact that I suffer from a food addiction, that shouldn't surprise you…

"Falling in love causes our body to release a flood of feel-good chemicals that trigger specific physical reactions," said Pat Mumby, PhD, co-director of the Loyola Sexual Wellness Clinic and professor, Department of Psychiatry & Behavioral Neurosciences, Loyola University Chicago Stritch School of Medicine (SSOM).[9] "This internal elixir of love is responsible for making our cheeks flush, our palms sweat and our hearts race."

MRI scans indicate that love lights up the pleasure center of the brain. When we fall in love, blood flow increases in this area, which is the same part of the brain implicated in obsessive-compulsive behaviors.

---

[9] https://www.sciencedaily.com/releases/2014/02/140206155244.htm

"Love lowers serotonin levels, which is common in people with obsessive-compulsive disorders," said Mary Lynn, DO, co-director of the Loyola Sexual Wellness Clinic and assistant professor, Department of Obstetrics & Gynecology, SSOM. "This may explain why we concentrate on little other than our partner during the early stages of a relationship."

Doctors caution that these physical responses to love may work to our disadvantage.

"The phrase, 'love is blind' is a valid notion, because we tend to idealize our partner and see only things that we want to see in the early stages of the relationship." Mumby said. "Outsiders may have a much more objective and rational perspective on the partnership than the two people involved do."

I once fell for a guy who was older than I. Even though I knew his age, his youthful look impressed me. Especially how little gray hair he had. You can imagine how shocked I was to learn he colored his hair. What? You already knew that? If I'd had my rational brain on, I too would have acknowledged that he held a 'Just for Men' loyalty card. But I was under his spell and couldn't see the truth in front of me. This a silly example, and coloring his hair is obviously not some sort of character flaw, but it shows how those chemicals released by love can really scramble our brains.

So, you get it. Love really is a drug. It feels wonderful but it can also feel devastating. My first crush was in the second grade. His name was Chad. I gave him a picture of me for his cubby. He returned it. I was seven years old and experienced my first heartbreak. The first of many, as it turns out, and it hurts just as bad whether you are seven or 77.

If I were vengeful, I might list some of the culprits here. The assholes who led me on, who lied, or who just weren't that into me. But they don't deserve that kind of recognition. It doesn't really matter who they are. We all have our own hurtful experiences. We might get over some of them sooner than others, but we shouldn't discount the pain. If we can take away a lesson, that's a bonus.

I'd like to think I've learned a thing or two about heartbreak over the years. I'm not saying this is something to be proud of, but if my experiences serve to ease your heartache a little, then I say, let's do it.

Looking back, the situations that hurt the most were the ones that were very wrong to begin with. Weird, huh? It could be because the right people work hard to avoid hurting us, or because we put so much more effort into trying to make something work that we shouldn't, that when it doesn't work out, that effort and emotion come crashing down like a heroin withdrawal.

Remember all those chemicals that were triggered when you fell in love? Heartbreak leads to a surge in cortisol and epinephrine in the body. And guess what happens then? An overabundance of cortisol tells your brain to send too much blood to your muscles, causing them to tense up, ostensibly for swift action. But you're not leaping anywhere, and as a result you're plagued with swollen muscles causing headaches, a stiff neck and an awful squeezing sensation in your chest.

It gets worse. A study published in the *Journal of Neurophysiology* found activity was induced in the part of the brain that also registers physical pain when participants were shown pictures of their exes. This is because emotional and physical pain share neural pathways in the brain. Your brain is signaling to your body that a breakup actually hurts.

Dr. Gabriella Farkas is a psychiatrist and founder of Pearl Behavioral Health, a center that provides evidence-based telepsychiatry and digital behavioral health services. She broke this down a bit further and put it in relatable terms:

"As time passes, activity in the attachment centers of the brain decreases, helping you move past the breakup. Thinking about your past relationship (looking at a pictures or social media, remembering 'the good times,' etc.), activates subcortical brain regions related to addiction, making such thoughts rewarding. The same reward systems control many drives including those connected to romance and food; the empty feeling after a breakup makes you want to fill it up, which explains comfort food.

"After pain and anger, being withdrawn and lethargic is common. Your brain and mind are trying to recuperate, like healing a wound. Attachment and love are survival-based emotional needs. From an evolutionary perspective, sadness, crying, etc., are symptoms meant to address the problem and promote seeking a new relationship to reproduce and continue our species. In terms of larger-scale physiology, chest pain and shortness of breath can result from the adrenaline and stress hormone rush following a breakup; it actually "stuns" your heart temporarily."

A study by David Buss, a fellow at the Center for Advanced Study in the Behavioral Sciences[10] has found evidence that an idealistic perception of someone can be harder to part with than the truth.

---

[10] http://onlinelibrary.wiley.com/doi/10.1111/j.1467-6494.1992.tb00981.x/full

According to Dr. Farkas, "Essentially, the good memories of a relationship make breaking up more difficult than the bad memories promote the breakup, because they are more salient in your mind.

"Negative aspects of the person/relationship are largely based on uncertainty and expectancies of the person's behavior. The more certain one is about their partner, the more loyal and devoted one will be to them. Yet when that illusion is shattered by deception or betrayal, interaction decreases, uncertainty increases, and the struggle to break-up intensifies. This *perceived* certainty/closeness is also a stronger predictor of emotional distress post-breakup."

But wait—there is good news!

Dr. Farkas adds, "With time, the attraction and nostalgia will fade, and you can move on to someone new!"

I've included this research to point out that you are not alone. You're not crazy for feeling pain and in fact you have no control over it. Or do you? You can't always control your automatic responses, but there are definitely things you can do to recover and get yourself to a good place.

Avoiding Heartbreak

I can't say that I've totally mastered this one. There are some people to whom we are drawn, and sometimes we just have to go through the experience to get us to the next phase.

If a guy (or girl) is interested in you, you know it. Remember the book, "The Rules?" I call BS on it. Waiting for three days after a date to call—that's for people playing games, not for someone looking for a real relationship. If a guy likes you, he'll call. He might text or communicate in another digital way, but he will reach out. Watch the movie, "He's Just Not That Into You," and you'll get a pretty good perspective.

I've broken my own heart as well. Remember earlier when I mentioned Mark Manson's article, "Fuck Yes or No"? The premise is that for a relationship to work, it needs to be a Fuck Yes for everyone. That doesn't mean get married and have babies. It does mean that both people need to be at the same enthusiastic level of commitment. Over time I've embraced this, which means shutting down situations when the other person wasn't all in. That can hurt. Also, remember that even if someone is "Fuck Yes" for you, you have to feel the same. It's so easy to love being loved. But if you don't reciprocate, that can be just as painful and lead to more unhappiness than heartbreak (sigh).

Getting Over It

If someone tells you to just get over it and move on, I give you permission to punch them. Sure, they mean well, but really. You can't just get over it. Your heart was shattered in a million pieces and you need a Roomba the size of the moon to pick them all up. But you can heal, and the pain will fade eventually.

Here are some tips:

Feel the pain. Take time to feel it. If you block it out, it could come back when you least expect, like at the grocery store or on an airplane. This might still happen, but give yourself a proper mourning period. You can't avoid the feelings, so you may as well face up to them sooner rather than later.

Give yourself a deadline. Wait, you thought I said that you can't just get over it. Correct, but you aren't going to wallow for long. What's reasonable? A week, a month? Pick a time, and when that day comes, put on your big girl/boy pants and rejoin the world. You aren't going to find a new partner with bags under your eyes and a chip on your shoulder. Go out on a few dates, hang out with friends or go visit kittens at the animal shelter. Just don't dwell.

Guided meditation and hypnosis. This isn't for everyone, but it can be powerful. I'm not saying to go out and hire someone as your personal guide, unless you have a lot of disposable income. If you do have some extra cash, find a professional in your area and give it a shot. If you are curious, but don't want a lot of expense, there are apps that you can download and listen to before bed or whenever you have a quiet moment. They give you exercises that help retrain your brain and change your association to the person. In fact, they are good not only for healing, but putting yourself into a mindset to attract the right things in your life.

Start dating. It might sound like a cliché, but meeting someone new can ease the pain of heartbreak. It doesn't work 100 percent of the time, but getting out there and finding someone who is totally into you can make you forget whatshername. Rebound sex can do wonders for your memory and your...ahem.

Don't hate them. After a breakup, hate is a very common emotion. Hate requires a lot of energy. It can be exhausting. Bitterness and resentment can eat away at you and make you less attractive to the right person. And ultimately, it will make you very unhappy. Resist the urge to hate. And if you can't, go take a boxing class, or hit a punching bag. Do whatever you have to do to get it out of your system.

Looking Back

Many of us have been in not-so-good to downright awful relationships, that we've thought about afterwards or given a second chance. We've all gotten into a fight with somebody and made up. That's not what I am talking about. I'm talking about opening up an entirely new chapter on a former love. Because there's always a possibility that you missed something the first time around, right? Maybe your timing was off, or you didn't have the maturity to make it work. Or perhaps you met a great person and started dating too young without the opportunity to experience life or see other people. Who knows—they might have been "the one" the whole time. Fairy tales do come true. Occasionally.

But it's not very likely.

Personally, I've never reunited with an old boyfriend and had it work out. Once I had a fairly decent relationship with someone with whom I had things in common and whose company I genuinely liked. However, something was always missing, and I wasn't happy. He wasn't affectionate with me and definitely did not know how to speak any of my love languages. He was an avid user of social media. He rarely mentioned me in his posts, although we dated for two years. You may think I'm being petty, but it bothered me. Was he ashamed of me? I am a fan of keeping private things private, but this was different. When he finally broke up with me, and I was pretty devastated. Keep in mind that I was fairly unhappy throughout the relationship, but still, I didn't want to end it.

I immediately started to date somebody else, which did not last very long and, upon ending that relationship, I tried to get back together with my ex. I then spent another two months of my life being even more unhappy by trying to fix a relationship that never worked.

Reflecting on it now, he was a jerk to me for our entire relationship. I made excuses for it and didn't want to see the big picture. Trying to get back together with him was a bad idea. The reason that it didn't work out the second time was because it was never gonna work the first time. And that's usually the way it goes.

When you're single, sometimes you go through the Rolodex of past relationships in your mind, rather than trying to find a new and better fit for you. Humans are comfortable with what is familiar, and we don't like change. Let's face it, the older you get, the harder it is to meet someone. It doesn't matter if you have a third eye on your head or if you are a supermodel—it is difficult for everyone, even Taylor Swift.

If you are flipping through your phone contacts wondering about calling McDreamy or texting McSteamy, stop and ask yourself. Did they make you happy the last time you were involved with them? Did they make you a priority? What were the challenges? Were they just not that into you? Were you just not that into them? If things were truly not right the first time, the chances of things being completely different the second time around are pretty slim.

Furthermore, going back to a bad situation from your past could mean missing an opportunity to start something wonderful with someone new who shows up in the present. I know, some of you are reading this and cursing me and my optimism. But seriously, talk to anybody who has found an amazing relationship after a hard break-up. They will probably tell you that the original break-up was a blessing, and that if it hadn't happened, they never would've met their current partner.

Still, it can be really hard to let go. I once was involved with someone for many years. We had almost gotten married, but in the end he was the wrong person, and our break-up dragged on forever. When we eventually fully ended things, I said to him, "We can still be friends." And I meant it.

Over time, we stayed in touch. It was superficial, but having cared about someone for a long time, I knew I didn't have to hate him. We would text on birthdays, and when my grandmother passed away, he came to the funeral. That meant a lot to me and my family. We never talked about any new relationships, although I knew he lived with someone.

One day, while looking for his business address on the good ole' internet, I stumbled upon his wedding registry and being human, I dug to see his wedding photos. Boom—dagger to the heart. What? Really? Why? We had been broken up for years, and I had moved on and was in a new relationship. In the words of Ms. Swift, we are never, ever, ever getting back together. So why did it hurt?

We shared a long time connection. We shared a home and a life, and those memories are deep-rooted in my psyche. I got confused and temporarily forgot about the reasons why we weren't together anymore. I had a moment, but then it passed.

This is normal, but it does take a lot of effort to get through all the layers of letting go. When moments like these happen, when you feel confused and off center about an ex, take a deep breath, and be thankful for the time you had together and the lessons that you learned from it, and send them wishes of happiness. No, don't go out and send them a vase from Tiffany's. Just mentally project positive vibes to them and go about being you. It takes a lot of patience with yourself.

Patience? Shut up, Jessica, you're annoying me.

This is unsolicited advice, remember? I never said that it was going to be easy, and whoever did is a complete liar. Relationships are complex, yes, but complex is not always a bad thing. Humans are not simple, and their many intricacies are part of what makes life so beautiful. You just might have to deal with some shit before you get to the beautiful part.

Finding Happily Ever After

We all have that friend who lists her relationship status on Facebook as "It's Complicated." This usually means that the significant other is married or not fully committed. I've been there—even if I never made it "Facebook Official." Complicated is not a relationship goal. Yes, on occasion, those super passionate, ultra-intense romances lead to happily ever after. Most of the time they don't. You want to know what works? Simple, *un*complicated relationships. The ones without drama. The ones that don't include exes in the mix. The ones that might even feel a bit boring, where you aren't blinded by love or in denial about someone's faults. We ALL have faults. Yes, honey, even I do. Faults are normal. Tears, angst, jealousy, that nagging feeling that something isn't kosher—that's not normal. Those are red flags. If you find yourself seeking advice on multiple aspects of your relationship, it might signal a problem.

Life is complex, but your relationship shouldn't feel like a roller coaster of emotions. Strong relationships include two adults working through the intricacies of their personalities to enjoy each other. They appreciate good times and act as a unit through any storms that arise.

Whether it's juggling family obligations and kids (shared or bonus), managing custody arrangements, handling finances or other challenges, they combine forces and tackle their shit together.

Not every relationship leads to marriage, nor should it. Dating different people helps us figure out what qualities we want in a long-time mate. However, if marriage is on your radar, understand that the wedding is just one day. Many divorced women admit they got caught up in the fairytale fantasy and quickly lived to regret it. That doesn't mean that happily ever after doesn't exist. On the contrary, choosing your spouse wisely, someone who consistently supports you, makes you laugh and is committed to sharing life with you is one of the best recipes for living the dream depicted in so many Disney movies.

Romantic love is one of life's greatest gifts. It can also be one of the most painful. We've all been there. Even after gallons of consolatory ice cream consumed with a side of tissues, I still choose love. I hope you do, too.

LESSONS FOR BEING HUMAN

1. Heartbreak is a real thing, with tangible, physiological symptoms, so give yourself the space to heal from it.

2. Healing from a bad relationship can be even worse than recovering from a good one, as we are forced to let go of the illusion of what it could have been.

3. It may sound trite, but it's true when it comes to love—time heals all wounds.

4. Ice cream and movies can help you through a bad break-up, but so can guided meditation and hypnosis.

5. Don't give in to hating an ex—it will hurt you more than him or her.

6. Looking back to old, failed relationships for another go-around is a tricky proposition. It can work, but the odds are usually against it.

7. Above all, don't lose faith—good love is worth the wait!

PUT THE YOLO IN YOUR SOLO

"Love yourself first, and everything else falls in line.
You really have to love yourself to get anything
done in this world."

– Lucille Ball

I decided that the best way to wrap up this book was to focus on some of the more pleasurable aspects of life. Of course, I could write a whole other book about all the things that give me pleasure, but let's save that for another time. For now, I'm going to start with the most top-of-mind things I know...

Taking Care of You

You all know the instruction they give to mothers on airplanes, right? In case of emergency, put your oxygen mask on first, and then put the mask on your child. The reason is, if you pass out for lack of oxygen, you won't be in a position to help anyone, and you'll both perish. Well, this logic applies to life in general. Self-care is fundamental to our ability to thrive. Because we're shooting for higher than just surviving, right? Since you've already come this far with me on this journey through my collected wisdom, here are some of the highlights of my approach to self-care...

Yoga is something that found me in my late 30s and yes, it might seem trendy, but its roots stem back to ancient India. The physical benefits are stellar, but the spiritual and mental aspects are transformative. It's a system of practices that includes breathing techniques, physical poses and meditations that help to calm and strengthen both the mind and the body. There are many different kinds of yoga, ranging from very challenging and athletic practices to forms that are geared especially for people with physical disabilities. For me, the real magic happened when I examined the history and philosophy behind it.

Understanding the connection between mind and body is powerful. I'm still trying to get there, but that is part of the journey. Don't take my word for it. Information about yoga is readily available online, where you can study the many different schools and approaches that have evolved over the centuries. Practicing yoga doesn't have to break the bank, either. Sure, you can take classes at fancy studios with instructors who have studied in India, but it can be done anywhere, anytime, even at home.

My first class was close to 10 years before I started practicing on a regular basis, and I absolutely hated it. I could not keep up, and while the rest of the class resembled graceful gazelles, I was as awkward as a circus clown. I realize now that most people are not that graceful either, and that the grace actually does come from practice. I also have come to understand that yoga is not about other people, but about yourself and pushing your own abilities. I've embraced another mindset—who the fuck gives a crap about what other people think? No one is looking at you and judging. If they are, then they are definitely missing the point of yoga and they're not focused on their own practice.

Yoga strengthens the mind as much as it does the body. It puts you in touch with your energy and works wonders for injuries. As someone who has suffered with chronic back problems, I can tell you that yoga stretches muscles and strengthens the core to prevent further back injuries.

But the psychological aspect shouldn't be dismissed. It helps to calm the breath and the mind, and increases one's ability to focus. In the best situations, yoga can be like a wonderful time-out, especially the part at the end called shavasana, where you basically lie on your back and rest.

Personally, I prefer hot yoga because my muscles are super tight from chronic inflammation, and the heat loosens everything up. I love sweating like crazy and leaving all the crap outside the room. It's like taking a mini vacation for an hour. The heat, the sweat, the practice of pushing yourself, it all melts the stress away.

The best instructors I've found are the ones who push you with compassion. In Mexico, I met a wonderfully gentle instructor. Having experienced an episode of inflammation, I pushed myself to attend class. I couldn't move very much and was frustrated. She helped me pose, and I was able to participate in the class without pain.

Balancing inner drive with practicality is what I love. My body just doesn't move in certain ways, but pushing to the limits of my ability is freeing. Having an in-person instructor is helpful, but if you can't afford a yoga studio, there are many YouTube videos available for free, and you can practice outside on the beach, at a park or even in your bedroom. There's a real physical benefit to hot yoga, but there's no reason to not do it in a room temperature environment and get an awesome benefit.

Yoga's not for everyone. I cannot get my boyfriend to go, even when I promise him a bacon cheeseburger at the end. I wouldn't say it's easy, either. It's challenging both mentally and physically, but the benefit it delivers is worth it.

Let's be very extravagant and talk about massage. Like yoga, massage has a physical and mental benefit. For stress management and the treatment of injury, it can change your quality of life. From an emotional standpoint, relaxing and shutting out everything going on in your life for an hour is intoxicating. Don't get me wrong—I've definitely had massage sessions when my brain wouldn't stop, and I thought, "Well that was a waste of an hour." But the physical part is there even if you can't get into an ultimate relaxation mode. Again, not everybody can afford to get a massage, but there are good deals out there. Membership clubs like Massage Envy or other subscription venues offer fairly reasonable options somewhere around $50 a month. I'm a huge fan of Groupon and have found deals close to $40 for a single massage. If you're stressed or in pain, a good massage can make a difference to your quality of life.

Peggy is a busy working mom. She has two personal commitments. One is getting a massage and the other is her standing hair appointment every six weeks. It's 45 minutes from her house and she uses that time to relax and enjoy herself.

She also orders from the personal shopping service, Stitch Fix. Not only is it like receiving a present in the mail, it saves her time having to shop.

Peggy is not alone in finding joy in saving time. A 2017 study[11,12] from the Proceedings of the National Academy of Sciences of the United States found that despite rising incomes, people around the world are feeling increasingly pressed for time, undermining their sense of well-being. The significance of the study is that the 'time famine' of modern life can be reduced by using money to buy time. Surveys of large, diverse samples from four countries revealed that spending money on time-saving services is linked to greater life satisfaction. The research shows working adults report greater happiness after

[11] http://www.pnas.org/content/114/32/8523.full
[12] https://www.nytimes.com/2017/07/27/science/study-happy-save-money-time.html?mcubz=0

spending money on a time-saving purchase than on a material purchase. People benefited from buying time regardless of where they fell on the income spectrum. There is a caveat that this may not hold true for the poorest of the poor. But if spending money on a personal shopper or having someone clean your house can decrease your stress, it might be worth it.

Even if you have no disposable income to spend on self-care, there are things you can do for yourself that cost no money. Spend a few minutes in the morning meditating or writing in a journal, reflecting on the things that make you feel grateful. Take a walk to get the cobwebs out of your head, or sit outside somewhere, to feel the sun or the breeze on your face. Prepare your favorite food and enjoy it. Take out a good book from the library, and get lost in it before you go to bed at night.

Regardless of whether it's a spa day, vacation, a long walk or run or mani/pedi or reading a book before bed, whatever works for you, take some time for self-care. Whether you're single or you have a bunch of kids, taking care of yourself is the most important thing you can do. Without self-care, you cannot take care of others to the best of your ability (remember the airplane rule).

Mirror, Mirror
In my family, makeup and fragrance were basic necessities. I practically came out of the womb wearing eyeliner. Recently, on the advice of some friends, I have focused much less on covering up my skin with cosmetics and have turned my attention to good skin care.

In the 1980s, Oil of Olay ran a campaign that always stuck with me. I was a young kid when it debuted and it influenced how I looked at aging. Today, its slogan, "I don't intend to grow old gracefully, I intend to fight it every step of the way," makes my head hurt. First of all, if we are lucky, we will grow old. Last I checked, it's a fact of life. Yet millions of women were encouraged to believe that the natural aging process lacked grace. Of course we want to take care of ourselves, right? We want to stay healthy and feel good as long as possible. The ad had the right idea, it just missed the mark a bit. Skin is the body's biggest organ, and taking care of it is as important as exercising or eating right. It's much less about not growing old and much more about staying healthy.

However, If I wanted to give my younger self one piece of advice, it would be to wear sunscreen. I'm pretty fair skinned and grew up in Florida, going to the beach nearly every weekend. My days were spent applying copious amounts of baby oil on my skin, and I am paying for that as an adult. Such a fundamental part of self-care is preservation. I've spent an exorbitant amount of money trying to repair the damage to my skin that was caused by the sun. Not everybody can afford luxury department store brands of skincare products, and you probably don't need them. There are some basic things that anyone can do, regardless of your finances.

Washing your face each night before you go to bed will help your skin renew while you sleep, especially if you put on moisturizer. As you take off the physical dirt that you accumulated from the day, you remove the emotional shit, too. You shed the day when you clean your face, which gives you a fresh start in the morning. Moisturizer not only helps retain your skin's vitality, it will just make it feel better.

However, the real no-frills tip when it comes to skincare is hydration. Good old fashioned water. I suck at getting in the right amount of water each day, and find alternatives like drinking green tea or coconut water makes its easier. Coconut water contains sugars and is not necessarily the equivalent of water, but it is better than becoming dehydrated. Dehydration causes body pain and muscle shrinkage. It causes your brain cells to shrink, too, and impairs proper functioning of your mind.

There is an old adage that says, "Beauty is in the eye of the beholder." Physical beauty is subjective, and societal standards vary by culture, changing over time. Our physical presence influences many aspects of our lives, both positively and negatively. Some of this is tied to our DNA, but much of it is related to the vibe we radiate. Positivity. Energy. Kindness. These traits contribute to how attractive we are to others because beauty is really on the inside.

I don't have kids of my own, but I'm an aunt and take ownership in how my nieces view the world. During a recent visit, my two-and-a-half-year-old niece watched me put on makeup in the morning. She was delighted as I pretended to put blush and eyeshadow on her little face. She was so excited to have her own "lipstick," which was just the clear lip balm I received in the airline amenity kit. Oh what fun it is watching a child play dress-up! Completing her makeover, she exclaimed, "Beautiful!" in her cute baby voice. As adorable as it was, it occurred to me that at her young age, she already equates makeup with looking beautiful.

Does this mean that our own self-worth is completely tied up in our physical appearance? I don't think so. Our physical appearance and how we take care of our bodies is a small part of what determines our happiness. Some people truly enjoy wearing make-up and getting all dolled up. It makes them happy.

No one should determine what brings someone else joy. The tricky part is ensuring that wearing cosmetics and paying attention to our physical appearance are both for our own pleasure and not just to make someone else happy. If you hate wearing makeup, if you do or don't want to color your hair, if you're a man who wants to wear a dress or a woman who likes to wear glitter, do it if it makes you happy. Wear the glitter and own it, because it's nobody else's business.

However, there is a caveat. You've figured out that life is complicated, right? You should feel empowered to do all of the things that bring you joy, but know that others may have opinions, and you have to be prepared for unsolicited comments. You have to be ready to accept the consequences of a harsh, critical world. Some days you might be ready to fully embrace this, to fully show the world who you are and with that, deal with the consequences. Just know that there could be other days when you are simply tired, when you just don't have the energy. And you know what? That's okay, too. You have to weigh which scenario will make you happiest.

On Monday, wearing your most outrageous hat could be the way to go. But on Wednesday, you might be dealing with a sick kid, or a boss who is dealing with her own shit and on that day, you might just decide that it's easier to be low key and not call attention to yourself. This is one of those wonderful things in life—we can be fluid. It's not that you must pretend to be someone you're not, it just means you can give yourself permission to take a day off once in awhile.

The Power of Music

Guess what? Music can have the same impact on the brain as food and love by releasing dopamine, according to scientists at The Montreal Neurological Institute and Hospital—The Neuro at McGill University. The team at The Neuro measured dopamine release in response to music that elicited "chills"—changes in skin conductance, heart rate, breathing, and temperature that were correlated with pleasurability ratings of the music. "Chills" (aka "musical frisson") are a well-established marker of peak emotional responses to music. A novel combination of PET and fMRI brain imaging techniques revealed that dopamine release is greater for pleasurable versus neutral music, and that levels of release are correlated with the extent of emotional arousal and pleasurability ratings. Dr. Robert Zatorre, neuroscientist at The Neuro, said: "These findings provide neurochemical evidence that intense emotional responses to music involve ancient reward circuitry in the brain."

Ok, enough science. The poet Henry Wadsworth Longfellow once wrote, "Music is the universal language of mankind." This statement is so powerful, that Andy Sharpe founded his company, SongDivision based on the premise of bringing the power of music to corporations around the world. Andy is a friend and client with whom I work closely. His passion for all things musical is contagious. According to him, "Life is better with music, and I'm lucky enough to have made a career sharing a form of expression that resonates with everybody."

He's right. Is there anybody who doesn't like music? Working with Andy and his team, I have seen first-hand how music can transform brand messages and corporate communication.

Applying Andy's theory that life is better with music, we can easily say that music acts as a tool for increasing positive thinking.

Do you have a theme song? A song that you go to when you are having a bad day or need to rally? The song you listen to before a test or before an interview?

Sometimes we need music to help set the tone for the day or help us come back from a high or a low.

Music is a great conversation starter. It can help you find commonalities with people or find the words when you don't have them in you.

One of my favorite activities is attending concerts. The feel of dancing and singing with a crowd of people is energizing. In fact, this whole section originated at…you guessed it…a Taylor Swift concert.

The title of the chapter, however, came to me during a show when Dustin Lynch sang "Why Not Tonight" with lyrics that say, "It's a solo full of YOLO." With a beer in hand, swaying away, fully appreciating the evening and the sounds, the words made me giggle as I took them in. You only live once, so if music lights you up inside, then make sure you keep plenty of it in your life!

Music makes it easier for me to deal with shit. I have a few theme songs for different occasions. I'll tell you what they are—but don't judge me. My personal mix includes Katy Perry's "Firework," Taylor Swift's "Shake it Off" and "Spotlight" by Madonna. This is a totally different list than my go-to karaoke song, "Don't Stop Believing" by Journey. It's a cliché, but I love it, because everyone sings along and they don't have to hear my awful vocals.

LESSONS FOR BEING HUMAN

1. Make self-care a priority! You can't take care of others if you don't take care of YOU.

2. Consider adding yoga or some other form of physical exercise to your self-care regimen, to keep your body toned and strong. It helps relax the heart and mind, too.

3. If you can afford it, spend a little money on a massage or other type of personal pampering.

4. Give yourself a free luxury of a long walk, a good library book or some time sitting in a relaxing place by yourself.

5. Stay hydrated! Water nourishes your entire body and helps your skin look its healthiest.

6. Wear (or don't wear!) whatever clothing or make-up you like.

7. Allow the power of music into your life, to transform your spirits and lift your soul.

EMBRACE YOUR SHIT

"The key to life is accepting challenges.
Once someone stops doing this, he's dead."

– Bette Davis

Here's what you do when you don't find the rainbow's end this time. Here's where you go when it looks like the rain won't end. Don't cry. There's always tomorrow, where you can have a second chance. And after tomorrow, all that you have to remember. Here's what you do when you think nobody cares for you.

Look in my eyes and see there's an answer there. It's true. We'll find tomorrow, a place for us. I know because time only knows how long forever's gonna last. Let's live today and find someone to share it with, because we only have one life to live.

So that's my parting unsolicited advice. No, no. Wait. That's not it. Those are the cheesy lyrics from the 1989 theme song to the soap opera, "One Life to Live."

There's always tomorrow. Or is there?

While it feels like we live in a time of uncertainty, you might as well make the most of life every day. The only thing that you have control of is how you handle what is thrown at you. That's it.

When asked why I wrote this book, my only answer is that it was a calling. The journey taught me things about myself and people that I wouldn't have discovered otherwise. It's my sincere hope that it helps others get by a little easier. Take all of the advice in this book, one piece that resonates with you, or use it as a guide for making the choices that are right for you.

Here are some parting lessons I want to share with you:

1. Be positive and manifest good shit like it's your job.
2. Be kind, but never a pushover.
3. Smile more.
4. Increase your competence.
5. Understand your capacity.
6. Have confidence.
7. Take care of your body and your soul.
8. Trust your gut.
9. Know your boundaries, and don't let people cross them.
10. Push yourself out of your comfort zone.
11. Just Love Life.
12. When the shit piles on, put on your theme song.
13. Be your own superhero.

Remember, we are all human and everyone has shit!

SOLICITED ADVICE

**"You know how advice is.
You only want it if it agrees with what
you wanted to do anyway."**

– John Steinbeck

Congratulations, you've made it to the bonus chapter. Woo hoo!

Wanting to include a wide variety of advice and snippets of wisdom, I surveyed people from all walks of life and asked them to share the best piece of advice they have for their fellow humans. I sifted through some of the best responses and am sharing them here. Have fun picking through this little candy bowl of sweet wisdom. Choose your favorites and leave the rest:

Damon Nailer, motivational speaker, author, life coach:
"Life is a game of adjustments; may the best adjusters win. One of the most vital components needed to live a successful, fulfilled and happy life is flexibility. This element is needed to offset as well as balance out the unpredictability of life. In pursuing various endeavors and functioning in many arenas, most of my goals I achieved weren't obtained when and how I thought they would be. However, because I made the appropriate adjustments, I ultimately achieved the majority of them and this concept can be applied in basically all areas of our lives."

Teresa Hogenson, marketing associate:
"Adaptation is the key. We find ourselves in many new situations in life and in work. Dealing with people, roles and new situations. The key is adaptation. That doesn't mean change to fit the situation, it means to adapt to fit the situation. Find your space where you can still be you without causing ripples."

Allen Klein, author:

"I am the one who puts a meaning on everything in my life. Nothing that happens to me has any inherent meaning. I am the one who assigns a meaning to everything. I can determine, for example, that not getting a job I wanted is the most awful thing in the world or I can see it as just a step to getting the most perfect job in the world."

Renea Hanks, global business consultant:

"Know your value and set boundaries."

Carol Gee, university administrator, author:

"You can never go wrong by going the extra mile."

Sandy Sandler, entrepreneur:

"Use a 5 minute journal every morning when you get up.[13]"

Joanna Douglas, owner of a cleaning service:

"Life is like a river, there are steady and rough streams. In order to get through the rough streams alive, you have to go with the flow."

Rachel Anevski's mother:

"Nothing too too good or too too bad lasts too too long."

Joe Rotella, smartest guy I know:

"Look for the intersection of your passion, what you're good at, and where there's opportunity. If you don't like the size of that intersection, work to grow it by focusing on those three areas. When you're working in that intersection, you'll be happy, succeed and feel fulfilled."

---

[13] https://www.safertech.com/product/five-minute-journal/

Paul Salinger, event marketer and mentor:
"Life? Live it, you've only got one shot. Don't waste time on unimportant stuff."

Jenni Fleck Jones, marketer:
"Don't borrow trouble."

Tom Morrison, author, speaker:
"100% of you living the life you want is directly connected to your goals, disciplined habits and persistence. Pursue wisely."

Miguel Neves, marketer and entrepreneur:
"Plant trees. Plant trees of love by investing quality time with your loved ones. Plant professional trees by creating long term sustainable value for your employers, partners and for yourself. Plant trees for yourself by investing in yourself every day. Wherever you go, keep planting trees."

Jamie Jablonowski, nurse and health coach:
"You deserve everything you've ever wanted. Don't let anyone ever convince you otherwise."

Amber Marlow, photographer:
"You might as well go for what you want."

Paul Coppinger, CEO:
"Run toward your fear."

www.ingramcontent.com/pod-product-compliance
Lightning Source LLC
Chambersburg PA
CBHW071229290326
41931CB00037B/2455